The
Salon
Owners
Bible

Simon Lotinga & Julie Eldrett

THE SALON OWNERS BIBLE

CONTENTS

TESTIMONIALS

EXACTLY WHAT I NEEDED

"This book is exactly what I needed. I've spent the last year learning how to develop systems for my salon and market consistently, but I struggled so much to find a format that I could work through. This book has helped me to put it all together."
MARIA GOAD ... TANGLES

IT WORKS

"I'd recommend this book to any salon owner, simply because it works. The way it's written makes it easy to follow. The language is chatty and friendly. I never once felt overwhelmed ... instead I found wow after wow!"
LOUISE BROSNAN _ ENVY HAIR & BEAUTY SALONS

REFRESHING

"It's so good to get a new and refreshing look at how things can be done differently."
ALISON LAWS _ JESMOND BEAUTY CLINIC

EUREKA

"This book is very easy to read and hard to put down because each page has its own Eureka moment!"
KEVIN BOYLE _ KB HAIR

Like Reading My Life Story

"It was like reading my life story. By page 9 my emotions were flowing, because running my salon takes so much out of me. Reading this book has given me the drive to finally make the changes that will give me a life outside work."
Alison O Sullivan – O Nails and Beauty

It Just Makes Sense

"Reading this book made me realise where I'm going wrong which is great because I'd got to the stage of either giving up or getting help and my first help is this magnificent book ... it just makes sense!"
Gillian Harkness – Academy Health and Wellbeing

Easy To Follow

"I enjoyed the fact that the book is so easy follow and the content isn't overwhelming!!! It will help me take my team and the salon forward and I'd definitely recommend it to other salon owners!"
Sinead Kelly – Precious Hair Design

SIMPLE BUT EFFECTIVE

"This book is a great way to take a fresh look at your salon and implement simple but effective ideas that have the power to achieve momentous change. The experience of the authors is evident throughout."
CHARLOTTE FALKENAU – SEGAIS HAIR AND BEAUTY

ANSWERS YOUR QUESTIONS

"This is a great book, because it's so easy to read and follow. It covers everything you want and need to know and you'll find it answers your questions clearly and concisely."
JOHN BAKER – DHD

ALL THE INFORMATION YOU NEED

"Two great people, one great book, so many pennies dropped. All the information you need and so much more!"
KIRSTY BEST – ODYSSEE

DEDICATIONS

You can't do what we do, for as long as we've been doing it, without learning from a lot of incredible people on the way.

Julie wants to dedicate her contribution to this book to her salon cast for trusting her and believing in her philosophies and ideas, because the results they achieved together gave her the confidence to travel the world sharing her experiences.

She says: *"We had great fun together so I thank everyone with all my heart... and you know who you are!"*

Julie would also like to say a very special **Thank You** to Michel Claire, who's the **International Professional Development Director**, for **L'Oreal Paris**, who has inspired her with his trust and integrity.

She says: *"Michel, my lifer is richer for knowing you and I'd like to thank you for the belief, support and opportunities you've given me."*

Simon would like to dedicate his contribution to everyone who's ever understood what he's been trying to say!

He'd like to give special thanks to his wife Sue who has put up with him getting out of bed most mornings at 5.30 to get the book finished.

He'd also like to thank the salon owners who were happy to share their stories and experiences in this book, because they knew it would make a difference and finally the authors, whose ideas have provoked the insights that make a book like this possible.

FOREWORD

"A number of years ago I received a phone call from Simon who is one of our customers saying he'd just written a book which mentioned my company Phorest because so many salon owners asked for his opinion about which salon software to use and he was very happy with the service we provided!"

"I asked to see a copy and was so impressed that over the years I've bought hundreds of books and given them as gifts to my customers."

"Simon and now Simon and Julie have gone on recommending us in subsequent books without ever asking for anything in return and I thought it was about time we repaid the compliment by putting into print our respect and appreciation for the help they've given to a group of people we as a company are also passionate about serving, namely Salon Owners."

"Running a salon can be a lonely business but as you're about to discover, the practical wisdom you'll find on every page of this enjoyable book really can make building a successful salon, so much easier for you. We can say this with confidence because, just like Simon and Julie, we know the key to long term success is retaining loyal clients."

Happy reading

Ronan Perceval: Founder & CEO Phorest Salon Software

INTRODUCTION

The Salon Owners Bible **is a big title.** It's a title that suggests a thought provoking book with wisdom in its pages and we hope that's what you discover!

It's also a title that suggests a book which has the answers to big questions.

Questions like:

- WHY does my salon exist?

- WHY should my staff choose to work with me, stay loyal to me, or care about me and my business enough to invest their careers in helping me grow it?

- WHY should a customer choose my salon to care about, be loyal to, to become a raving fan of?

If you've never asked yourself questions like these, you're going to love this book. If you have, but found them too difficult to answer ... **you're going to love it even more!**

Why?

Because by the time you've finished reading it you'll know WHY your business exists and WHY your staff and customers should care and stay!

You'll also know HOW to take the answers and use them to create a different sort of salon. A salon that makes a DIFFERENCE in people's lives ... especially YOURS.

Finally you'll know WHAT practical steps you need to take to make your WHY and HOW come alive.

That's our promise. That's WHY this book exists. We've written it with passion because growing salons we define as **'successful'**, thrive in the long term and give their owners the life, lifestyle and purpose that makes it all worthwhile, is <u>our</u> purpose in life. We both feel it's what we were put on this earth to do and we find it profoundly satisfying when the ideas we share make a difference.

In other words we exist to help you discover answers to many of the problems that have been holding you back for years. We exist to provoke inspiring 'aha' ideas or thoughts that change the way you see your salon, its purpose and what it can achieve ... *for ever.*

We use words like **'discover'** and **'provoke'** quite deliberately because there is no one single **'right'** way to run a salon.

Why not?

Because we're all different! Our difference means it's impossible to have **ONE** right answer but there <u>**are**</u> principles that point you in the direction of finding **YOUR** right answer.

Some of these principles will be obvious to you and you could be using them already. Others will be hiding from you in plain sight, which means they're <u>**always**</u> there ready and waiting to help you, but at the moment you just can't see them for what they are.

The answers you're looking for.

This means, it makes sense to go through this book with an open mind. When you do, you'll discover plenty of things you're familiar with and almost certainly some ideas that challenge you.

We want you to take comfort from the familiar, BUT BE AWARE, if your salon isn't thriving, if it's causing you stress and problems, if it isn't giving you the life and lifestyle you really want ... **the familiar is obviously not enough.**

This means you'll find the answers to YOUR challenges in the ideas in this book that challenge YOU!

The familiar has got you to where you are now. If this is not where you want to be, then be prepared to look into your unknown, be prepared to leave your comfort zone, be prepared to try some new answers on for size!

With that said, let's get started by imagining for a moment that creating a successful salon is a lot like completing a jigsaw puzzle.

You may be wondering what we mean ... so think about it like this.

A jigsaw puzzle usually comes with a picture on the lid, doesn't it?

Why?

Because it makes your puzzle so much easier to fit together when you know what it's supposed to look like!

Having a powerful reason WHY your salon exists gives you a picture to work towards, in the same way.

It helps if you plan HOW you're going to fit your puzzle together before you start as well, doesn't it. Having a clear strategic plan in place helps your salon come to life in just the same way.

With a picture to work from and a plan to guide you, seeing WHAT pieces need to go where becomes pretty obvious, doesn't it ... **the same logic applies to your salon.**

In a perfect world every salon would have a big clear ...

- WHY picture
- HOW strategy and
- WHAT plan

But what happens if it doesn't?

What happens if some of your pieces are missing, or they get mixed up with pieces you've borrowed from another salon owner's puzzle because you saw what they were doing and thought... **that's what I've been missing!**

Worse than that ... what happens if you lose your picture on the lid or you haven't even got one?

You might get confused, downhearted and give up. You might get frustrated, angry and take it out on everyone around you. It all depends on your character and personality, but whatever happens it's going to cost you time, energy and money to sort everything out, isn't it, and this begs a question.

How much time, energy and money can you afford to waste before you get it right?

It's your life ... you get to choose!

Research shows us that **10%** of salon owners have got their jigsaw puzzle together beautifully but that means ... **90% have got missing bits, mixed up bits, or no picture on the lid.**

To be fair **10%** are pretty close and **20%** are trying hard. This leaves **40%** who are getting by and **20%** who might be better off doing something else!

So here's a question ... two questions in fact.

1. Which group of salon owners do you belong to now?
2. Which group would you like to belong to?

We know from our experience as salon owners, coaches, mentors, consultants, speakers, authors, trainers and human beings, that the **20%** who need the most help won't ask for it, which saddens us, but it's true.

We also know the **40%** who are only getting by won't read this book from cover to cover either... **so if you do, it means you're almost certainly in the top 40% which suggests:**

- You're either there already, but realise there's always something new to learn.

- Nearly there and just want to make sure you're on track.

- Trying hard to get there, but it's just taking a bit longer than you wanted it to!

The good news is that it doesn't matter which part of the top **40%** you're in at the moment, this book is for you.

Does that sound good?

If it does, then we're ready to get started and let's start by introducing the 'we' you'll see us referring to all the way through the book.

We are **Simon Lotinga** and **Julie Eldrett** and anyone who knows us will tell you we're very different personalities, with very different career paths who, after more than 80 years of combined salon experience, have ended up coming to exactly the same conclusions about what it _**really**_ takes to create a successful salon.

We began to notice that we believed in the same principles, when we were both invited to be part of the **Matrix** business education team. We'd be on stage together from time to time and we'd find ourselves nodding and agreeing with each other.

So far, so good ... but it was only when we shared a 3 hour car journey together and had the time to talk in depth about our beliefs, that it became glaringly obvious how much we agreed on **'The 3 BIG Steps'™** that form the fundamental, basic, non-negotiable foundations that have to be there in any salon if long term success is going to be achieved and maintained.

If you've attended any of Julie's courses you'll know her story.

How she became a salon owner as a franchisee for a large group. How some very difficult personal challenges made her a stronger person, better able to deal with life's ups and downs.

How she thought that the other franchise salon owners must be doing better than her because of the cars they drove and what they said at meetings about how well their salons were performing.

Her shock at being invited to head office to explain why her customer satisfaction figures were so high.

How her second career opened up, when she was invited to share her **'Customer Care'** secrets with the other franchise holders. How her success at this led to invitations to speak to other salon owners all over the UK and regular invitations to write columns in fashion and business magazines.

How the world started to notice she had something special to share, which led to her current jet setting existence with invitations to travel, teach and speak all over the world. You'd be amazed how much of Julie's contribution to this book was written in places like India, Mexico and China!

As for Simon, if you've read either of his books you'll know how, after cutting his salon teeth in his father's business, he joined L'Oreal as a field Technician and then Technical manager.

How he had a team to work with and the pleasure of being able to go into hundreds of salons a year, not only to help them with their technical development, but also more and more as time went on, with their business problems as well. This was definitely a sign of things to come!

How driving 50,000 miles a year, staying away from home 3 or 4 nights a week and company politics, persuaded him to retire from 'corporate' life, become the master of his own destiny and open his own salon.

How **'the big mistake'** that trips up most salon owners, made his first 5 years an unhappy time. Unhappy because it left him feeling trapped with constant staff, time and money problems.

How the problems were caused because he was too busy doing hair to stand back and see what was really happening.

How he tried all sorts of quick fixes like giving pay rises, holding staff motivation days, refitting his salon, introducing new product lines, holding **'in salon'** seminars with big name stylists and so on.

How each initiative cost time and money and things would appear to improve ... but it was an illusion, the effects didn't last.

How one day he reached his **'Sod It'** point and started looking for answers outside the world of salons and because of this he gradually understood what was wrong and what he could do about it.

How his staff problems began to melt away as the group of people who'd caused so many problems started working well together. How, in spite of the recession at the time, his money problems began melting away as well, as he finally understood how to take control of a salon and make it profitable.

How he became ill and his doctor told him; *"You've got to have 6 months off!"*

How he went back to the salon and with no notice called a staff meeting and said, *"I've got to have 6 months rest, you're going to have to run the salon for me"*. How they panicked, but he pointed out ... *"you've actually been running it for the last year or so!"*

How his team accepted the challenge and when Simon went back 6 months later, they'd absorbed his column,

.

and actually grown the business. Salon turnover had increased in spite of the fact that he wasn't there ... and they didn't even take on another stylist to replace him!

Would that happen in your salon if you took 6 months off with no notice?

The rest of his story is history. He wrote a booklet about his experience and other salon owners became interested in what is now known as *'The Successful Salon System'*™.

Requests for coaching, mentoring and running courses followed.

In spite of a hectic schedule, as he tried to be everywhere at once, salon owners still wanted more from him. The obvious answer was to write a book, so *'The Seven Most Expensive Mistakes Salon Owners Make'* was published. When the recession turned the world of business as we know it, upside down, *'The Salon Owners Guide To beating The Recession'* was his answer.

With the benefit of hindsight it looks like all the work they've both done until now has just been preparation, because these two wise and experienced souls have decided to channel their passion for empowering salon owners to create successful, profitable, easy to run salons, into a new business.

It's a business with a real purpose ... to make **'The 3 BIG Steps'**™ the industry standard as the natural and obvious way to create, organise and run a successful salon. This is a business that has asked the big WHY questions we gave you at the beginning of this chapter ... **and found the answers.**

It's a business that has a big HOW strategy and a big WHAT plan as well.

So now you've been introduced to your two authors and the fundamental WHY, WHAT, HOW structure of **'The 3 BIG Steps'™** that are at the heart of every salon we've ever seen that's enjoyed sustained long term success, we'd love to show you how you make them come alive in your salon.

Let's start with a statement of the blindingly obvious.

A salon is nothing ... NOTHING ... NOTHING without people, in fact its sole purpose is to serve people.

- You're a person ... so it needs to serve you.
- Your team are people ... so it needs to serve them.
- Your customers are people ... they are very important too!

As salon owners we don't exist in a vacuum. We are part of an interconnected world and at its heart and the very heart of our existence are the laws that govern human nature.

We're talking about our nature, the nature of the people we employ, the nature of the people who we want to attract and keep as long term loyal raving fan clients.

Human nature is what it is and we have to understand the fundamental truth of this and work with it, but the sad fact is up to **90%** of the salon owners we meet in our work are ignoring or fighting it instead and this is causing most of their problems!

So let's get personal and specific, shall we.

If **you** want to enjoy long term success in **your** salon you're going to have to create a business that works with human nature **AND** at the same time is well organised and profitable.

So how can we make this apparent contradiction work?

How can we get salon owners, employees and customers, with very different emotions, thoughts, beliefs, habits, values, experiences and needs to come together in a way that's predictable, consistent, emotionally satisfying and profitable, to create a successful salon?

Can it actually be done?

Of course it can ... by following the **'The 3 BIG Steps'™** and using them as your compass point to guide you in everything you do.

Chapter 1

Why + How = What a Great Salon!

As you've learned the purpose of this book is to make the **'The 3 BIG Steps'™** come alive for you and in this chapter we want to help you understand where their power comes from.

It may surprise you.

Before we go into detail, it makes sense to start by looking at a great example of what we're talking about and we've chosen one of the world's most iconic companies ... **Apple.**

Whatever happens to Apple in the future now that **Steve Jobs** has sadly passed away, you can't deny the fact that their **iPads, iPods, iPhones** and **Apple Macs** have changed the way many of us live our lives.

But what makes Apple and their products stand out in a crowded market place?

Most people would say it's down to the genius of Steve Jobs and **Steve Wozniak** who founded Apple together in 1976 and quickly turned it into a huge success story.

How quickly?

Well, their annual turnover grew from a million dollars in 1977 to a billion dollars in 1983, which is stunningly quick growth by any standards.

With the benefit of hindsight we can look back and see that the foundation of their success was having a clear purpose.

In other words they knew WHY Apple existed ... and it wasn't just to make money!

At the time, computers were huge main frame devices that took up whole rooms, cost a lot of money and gave large companies and corporations who could afford them a big advantage in business.

The two men were the right people in the right place at the right time because Silicon Valley in 1977 was the birthplace of the Microcomputer and their big WHY was to create products that changed the rules, so small companies and individuals had the tools to compete with the giants.

Now you know this, it's suddenly obvious WHY Apple came up with so many innovations that changed what's possible for small companies and individuals like us, isn't it.

It's what the company was born to do.

Having a big WHY is only the first step though, because without an effective HOW to make it come alive a big WHY is just a dream!

So HOW did they do it? The answer to that question is by making sure they had a story their customers could tell **themselves and their friends** about WHY they buy Apple.

The story was simple.

Apple make beautifully designed easy to use products

that are different and choosing Apple says something about YOU!

Here's one small example of how they made the story come alive. When Steve Jobs first saw office machine manufacturer, **Xerox** demonstrate what we now call a computer mouse, it was complex and expensive. He saw the potential it had to change the way a microcomputer was used and reputedly went back to Steve Wosniak and said *"I want you to create a version that costs $15 dollars to make and is so versatile I can use it on any flat surface, including my jeans!"*

We take the mouse for granted now, don't we, but Apple was the company that saw what it could be.

They also made beautiful design an integral part of their products. Steve Jobs realised making them look cool and 'designed' rather than just functional would change how his customers felt about them ... and he was right.

What was the result of their insight in creating a story and bringing it to life?

Their customers connected with the company in a way their competitors couldn't understand. They couldn't understand because they were focussing on WHAT their products did (their features and benefits) and this difference in approach left the door wide open for Apple to stand out and thrive.

By 1984 their relentless progress was beginning to falter and they realised help was needed, so Jobs lured corporate superstar **John Sculley** who was president of **Pepsi** at the time to be their new CEO with the vision of creating a company together that changed the world.

Progress had slowed because some of the products Apple launched in the early 1980's didn't sell well. Once Sculley had settled in to his new role and started to get a clear idea what was needed, his relationship with Jobs came under strain because they didn't agree about the way forward.

In 1985 after a major disagreement about the cost of the flops and a strategy for dealing with them, Jobs called a board meeting and a summary of what he said would go like this; *"I want to invest in turning these failing products round ... Sculley says no ... I think you should back me!"*

Probably to his surprise they didn't. Instead they took away some of his responsibilities because they were concerned about his behaviour at the time.

It took a few months for him to make up his mind, but in the end the genius who'd done so much to create this amazing company resigned in disgust and the rest is history.

Without his vision and big WHY Apple lost its way and became locked in a battle to the death with Microsoft instead.

By 1996 they were losing money and customers at a huge rate and bankruptcy loomed.

At this point Jobs who'd gone on to build Pixar into a successful film animation company decided to step back in. The first thing he did was join forces with Microsoft and persuade Bill Gates to invest a badly needed $150 million dollars into Apple plus a 5 year commitment to create a Mac friendly version of the Microsoft Office Suite.

When asked why he agreed to come back, Jobs said, *"My DNA and Apple's DNA are completely intertwined. The Apple's brand is badly tarnished and I intend to restore it."*

He did that by restoring their focus on the Apple story about WHY being different matters and this allowed them to show the world once again HOW they were different and customers once again realised WHAT was so special about Apple and bought their products by the bucket load.

For Jobs it was a deeply personal effort as he worked to remind Apple's employees, its customers, and perhaps even himself of the story about what the company stood for. *"You can't talk about profit, you have to talk about emotional experiences"* he would say.

He was right!

You can read all about the lessons Apple has to teach in **Simon Sinek's** ground breaking book **'Start With Why'** which we'd highly recommend you do.

Read it and you'll discover he points to something that all great leaders and communicators seem to naturally understand.

People don't buy WHAT you do … they buy WHY you do it.

In other words … **they BUY the story of your WHY.**

He then explains that the natural sequence for messages that inspire people and get them to accept change, make decisions and take action is:

- WHY... *because it engages them emotionally.*

- HOW ... *because it gives them a path to follow and a choice they can make.*

- WHAT... *because it gives the logical reasons they need to rationalise the emotional decision they've already taken and feel good about it.*

Give your staff and customers a story of WHY to tell themselves and their friends and they'll fall in love with your salon and stay in love with your salon for as long as you stay true to the story and it remains relevant to them.

We admit that when we saw what Simon Sinek was saying in his book we found it compelling because we understood straight away that we'd both instinctively followed the WHY, HOW, WHAT sequence in developing our salons and it had underpinned our success.

Seeing the power of what we'd done *'by instinct'* in this totally new way got us really excited!

We both knew WHAT we'd done worked, but until we read Simon Sinek's book we didn't truly understand the human biology of WHY it worked.

We didn't understand that hearing an emotional WHY story triggers a biological response deep inside us to care, to trust, to get involved, to be loyal, to belong and there's a reason why it happens.

Back in the mists of time we had fairly primitive limbic mammal brains, but we were able to make basic decisions, be creative and experience emotions like trust, confidence, connection and loyalty.

What we didn't have was the ability to speak or think rationally and logically. This came later when our Neocortex developed and as a species we made the great leap forward.

In spite of this amazing addition to our brain capacity, the primitive limbic mammal part of our brains still exists.

It not only exists ... it still controls our ability to be creative, make decisions and feel emotions like trust, confidence, connection and loyalty!

It still does all this and it does it without the benefit of language to communicate with. Instead it generates feelings ... **emotional feelings that our rational, logical Neocortex interprets for us afterwards.**

This means we're wired up to make emotion based decisions, **BEFORE** we rationalise them with logic.

This explains why, when you try and influence people with WHAT based logical facts before giving them a WHY they find it hard to make a decision!

If you give people an emotion charged reason WHY they should listen you, you're automatically communicating with the part of the brain where decisions are made and feelings like trust, confidence, connection and loyalty are created.

Touch that part of us with a message that connects and we'll make a decision instinctively and then sift through the facts to find the logic we need to support the decision we've already made.

We've all done it, in fact we can't help ourselves and this was proven by some fascinating research we've seen that shows that humans can sometimes make decisions up to 10 seconds **BEFORE** we consciously think we've made it!

So now you know why it makes sense for you tap into the power of starting with an emotion based, reason WHY story about your salon.

Use it to explain WHY you're different, HOW you keep your promises and WHAT customers can consistently expect.

Use it because it leads your customers along the natural path of **WHY + HOW = What a great salon!**

Now, you're probably thinking ... **'what you're saying makes sense but I don't know my WHY and I certainly don't have an emotion based story to tell, so WHAT do I do?'**

The answer to that question is ... follow **'The 3 BIG Steps'™** and your journey begins in the next chapter!

CHAPTER 2

IT'S ALL ABOUT YOU!

Do you remember the big WHY questions from our introduction?

WHY does your salon exist?

WHY should your staff choose to work with you, stay loyal to you, or care about you and your business enough to invest their careers in helping you grow it?

WHY should a customer choose your salon to care about, be loyal to, to become a raving fan of?

The key principle of <u>Step 1</u> of 'The 3 BIG Steps'™ is creating an emotionally strong story with the power to connect with your staff and customers.

An emotionally strong story gives you your WHY.

Step 1 is the fundamental step. It's the step most salon owners trip over or miss out completely and if you subscribe to our blog **www.thesuccessfulsalonblog.com** you may remember that at the beginning of 2014 we conducted a survey that proved this is true.

We proved that something fundamental is being missed or tripped over in the majority of salons because:

- **52%** of the salon owners surveyed had problems caused by poor marketing.

- **63%** had problems caused by poor mind management.

- **41%** had problems caused by poor staff selection and management.

- **65%** had problems paying their bills.

- **64%** had problems getting their less experienced staff busy.

- **72%** said they were so busy running their salons that their personal life suffered because of it.

We'll come back to these results as we go through the book together but think about it ... we're talking about real salon owners and there has to be a reason why so many of them have problems like these to deal with, doesn't there.

Is it because salon owners who have problems are simply the victims of a lot of bad luck?

Bad luck happens, doesn't it, but could **so** many people be **that** unlucky, or is something else going on?

Logically, there has to be another reason and we say that reason is simply because salon owners find it difficult to get to grips with step one.

This means they don't have their own personal answers to the big WHY questions and there's a reason for this. If you want to know what it is ... **you'd better keep reading!**

We've been into thousands of salons between us and we've seen every staff, money and marketing problem you can imagine. We've noticed that particular problems seem to be attracted to salon owners with particular behaviour or personality types.

If this is true, *and we know it is*, then logically your personality and behaviour has a direct impact on your ability to answer the big WHY questions, which means, as far as the secret to creating a successful salon is concerned ...

It's all about YOU!

It also means if you want to find **your** answers to the big WHY questions you need to start with a health check on your personality and behaviour.

Simon wrote a whole chapter about this in his last book and we're going to borrow a simple set of questions he asked then and use them to gently introduce you to an idea that could dramatically lower the 'problem' scores we'd see if we were ever to conduct the survey again!

So assuming you want fewer problems, have a go at answering these questions.

With each one, just choose the number between 1 and 10 that reflects how strongly you feel ... *with 1 meaning* **DEFINITELY NOT** *and 10 meaning* **DEFINITELY!**

Take your time, think about them carefully and answer honestly.

Are you afraid of making mistakes?

Circle your score   1 2 3 4 5 6 7 8 9 10

Do you find it hard to say no?

Circle your score 1 2 3 4 5 6 7 8 9 10

Do you try to be perfect?

Circle your score 1 2 3 4 5 6 7 8 9 10

Do you expect perfection in others?

Circle your score 1 2 3 4 5 6 7 8 9 10

Do you often feel guilty?

Circle your score 1 2 3 4 5 6 7 8 9 10

Do other people let you down a lot?

Circle your score 1 2 3 4 5 6 7 8 9 10

Do you find it hard to trust?

Circle your score 1 2 3 4 5 6 7 8 9 10

Do you put other people on a pedestal and think they're better than you?

Circle your score 1 2 3 4 5 6 7 8 9 10

Do you worry about the future?

Circle your score 1 2 3 4 5 6 7 8 9 10

Are you a born sceptic?

Circle your score   1   2   3   4   5   6   7   8   9   10

How did you get on?

Did you score **4** or higher on any of the questions?

We're only asking because, before you'll be able to tell your story in a way that inspires people to join you in taking **'The 3 BIG Steps'™** you'll need a healthy, balanced self-image and a score of 4 or higher on any of these questions is a clear sign there's some **insecurity** lurking behind the scenes.

Insecurity is like emotional cancer.

It's often hidden but it sucks the positive emotion out of a salon by eating away at confidence, trust and your ability to connect to other people in a healthy way. Take trust, confidence and connection away from a salon and it will never **EVER** enjoy long term consistent success.

Insecurity is also the reason WHY so many salon owners find it hard to answer the big WHY questions.

Remember, if you've got no answers you'll have no inspiring, emotionally attractive story to tell.

Insecurity is also why **52%** of the salon owners we surveyed had problems caused by poor marketing ... **because the foundation of ALL great marketing is having an emotionally attractive story to tell!**

Now you can see why it's so important to get to grips with insecurity, can't you!

To do this, we badly need a basic understanding of human psychology and the role it plays in allowing insecurity and low self-esteem, to cause so much damage to our confidence, dreams and salons.

To begin with can we agree that you only know you're alive because your brain is creating thoughts?

Thoughts appear as if by magic in your head, don't they, but did you know that before you get to experience the full three dimensional, surround sound, sensory reality of a thought, it goes through your self-image filter.

This is your guide to the world and how you fit into it. **It's like having a 'Satnav' with a map of your beliefs about reality built into your head.**

Its job is to help you stand on your own two feet and function as an individual ... **and it only works properly if you have a secure identity.**

A secure identity automatically gives you self-esteem, a balanced self-image and the ability to trust, connect and feel confident. It also protects you from being overwhelmed by negative emotions like, guilt, jealousy, rejection or fear of failure.

Self-esteem and a balanced self-image are important psychological protection mechanisms and your ability to stay sane and emotionally healthy depends on them!

This is why your brain resists anything that doesn't fit with your identity or self-image once it's formed ... **it does it to protect you because it wants you to stay on the right road, sane and emotionally healthy.**

Having a built in **'Satnav'** to guide us through life sounds like a great idea, doesn't it ... but there's a problem.

Many of us end up with an insecurity virus infecting our 'Satnav' software. Do you remember our salon owners survey showed **63%** had problems caused by poor mind management... **and trust us, this figure is conservative!**

Most of the time your software works fine, but when your security is threatened or trust is needed, it has a habit of sending you off in the wrong direction and this can cause all sorts of problems as we'll see in a minute.

Just before we go there, you might be wondering how your **'Satnav'** software got a virus in the first place.

The answer is ... it happened as you grew up because unless you were very lucky, you were surrounded by people running **their** lives on virus infected software and you unknowingly picked it up from them!

To understand how, we want to introduce you to the **7 Stages of Emotional Development** which we should all naturally grow through as we develop from being a new-born baby into an emotionally healthy adult.

As we look at each stage we'll see it in its secure identity 'ideal' form first. Then we'll give you the tell-tale signs that show you what insecurity virus infected behaviour can look like!

By the way, we first learned about the 7 stages of emotional development from **Dr Michael Broder** and his excellent book **'Stage Climbing'** which is well worth reading if you want an in depth understanding, but for now we're going to share our understanding of his ideas and we think you'll be amazed at what you discover about human nature ... **especially yours!**

Stage 1: The 'Infant' Stage

In stage 1 *Dr Broder* explains that for the first 9 to 12 months of life, you were helpless. You relied on your parents for everything and if you were lucky, you were fed when you were hungry, cuddled when you were upset and your nappy was changed when you soiled it.

In other words, in an ideal world, every one of your emotional and physical needs was met.

As everything is done for you, you'd expect us all to progress naturally to stage 2 pretty easily, but not every baby is lucky enough to get what they need, when they need it. This can affect the development of their **'Satnav'** software and some people are quite capable of going back to stage 1 on a regular basis at any age in life!

How would you know if someone's gone back to stage 1?

Well the signs are actually quite obvious. You'd know because they find it hard to take responsibility. They avoid it by making excuses. When things go wrong they truly believe it isn't their fault.

They see themselves as victims with no control and often

hide behind procrastination or an inability to make decisions, preferring others to make them for them.

Do you know people who behave like this at times? Are they easy to inspire, work with, serve or motivate?

Can you imagine how well your salon would run if you regularly went back to any insecure stage 1 behaviour? It would be the cause of all sorts of problems, wouldn't it!

So to summarise: At stage 1 we don't have responsibility.

Now let's take a look at ...

Stage 2: The 'Toddler' Stage

Once you start to walk and talk, *Dr Broder* explains, you begin to see a world that's full of possibilities. You're naturally curious and you want to explore or play with anything and everything!

It's how you discover the way things work and what you like and don't like. The problem is, at this stage you have no boundaries. Life's all about you. You see it, you want it **... and you want it NOW!**

- You don't know what's right or wrong.

- You don't know if something's valuable or important.

- You have no concept of ownership, or time.

None of these things mean anything to you yet, so as you go through stage 2, your parents try and teach you **THEIR** limits and rules. We emphasise the word 'their' because each of your parents will have their own **'Satnav'** guiding them and they may not agree on the limits and rules. This can be very confusing for you as a child!

Anyway, as your parents do the best job they can to teach you, there's a good chance you'll throw some tantrums, because it takes a while to learn, understand and accept you can't have what you want, when you want it all the time.

How your parents handle your tantrums is very important, but if you're lucky and they get it right, you'll progress naturally to stage 3.

If you're not so lucky and your **'Satnav'** software has already picked up a virus from your parents by this stage, you'll find some people are quite capable of going back to stage 2 on a regular basis.

How would you know when they do?

Well it shows itself as behaviour that doesn't have boundaries. Because of this, stage 2 insecure people have problems with concepts like self control, truth, trust or integrity.

In its mild form stage 2 insecurity can show up as:

- Telling 'little white lies'.

- Gossiping and talking about people behind their backs.

- Thinking it's OK to take home low value items from hotel rooms or your place of work.

- Adult tantrums.

In its more extreme form you'll see people:

- Lying.
- Breaking promises or agreements.
- Being unfaithful.
- Stealing.
- Unconstrained violence.

Do you know people who exhibit any insecure stage 2 behaviour?

How would your salon perform if you regularly used insecure stage 2 behaviour? It would be a disaster, wouldn't it, because no one would trust you!

So to summarise: At stage 2 we don't understand boundaries.

Now let's take a look at ...

Stage 3: The 'Rule Abiding' Stage

Hopefully your stage two tantrums will drop away as you gradually learn some boundaries and see that behaving well makes life easier. This means you'll start to progress through Stage 3, which is characterised by feeling comfortable with rules, structure, order and avoiding conflict.

As you do, it would be rare for you to see yourself as unique, or a rebel. You're far more likely to want to conform, fit in and be part of a group.

A talent for art, music, writing, performing or sport may begin to appear and it's quite likely you'll start to understand that it's nice to help other people.

If your parents help you through this stage by providing loving guidance and appropriate discipline, you'll gradually develop a sense of your own uniqueness. You'll also start to feel it's OK to challenge rules that don't make sense to you anymore and your parents will discover that saying, *"because I said so"* no longer works in the way it used to!

As your sense of identity starts to grow you should naturally move on to stage 4 but a significant number of people never do.

Why?

Because they feel comfortable with rules so they have little motivation to grow beyond them.

How would you know if an adult is showing insecure stage 3 behaviour?

Clues will show up in one of two ways.

You'll either see them trying to be dominant, because they want to impose order, structure and compliance on anyone who will let them.

Or you might see submissive behaviour instead. It's a fact that some people are only happy when they are living in a world of structure, order and having someone tell them what to do, say and think.

For obvious reasons, organisations like the army, police and prison service, where rules, structure and discipline are part of their natural culture, prove very attractive to some stage 3 people. You'll find others joining cults, sects and religious groups that have very strong rules ... **but it's not that unusual to see some forms of stage 3 insecure behaviour popping up in salons.**

You'll see it if someone is being bossy and they only seem happy when they're telling other people what to do. Or you'll see it if someone only seems to function when they are told what to do.

Do you know people who behave like this?

What would happen in your salon if you became a stage 3 bossy tyrant when you felt threatened by anything? What would happen in your salon if you became a stage 3 submissive who was happy to be controlled and told what to do by other people who had a controlling streak in them?

It's pretty obvious what would happen. You'd either drive other people away or end up as the salon doormat!

So to summarise: At stage 3 we learn about fitting in.

Now let's look at ...

Stage 4: The 'Approval Seeking' Stage

We mentioned earlier that, as you move into stage 4 *which would be your teenage years*, you'll begin to feel it's OK to challenge rules that don't make sense anymore. As you do, you replace the need for rules with the need for acceptance and approval instead.

You want to be liked, respected and admired for who **you** are by the people whose opinion matters to you.

Because your parents, teachers and peers know you very well, they might not think you're quite as wonderful as you now want them to!

If this happens it's possible you'll rebel, break away or change direction and look for acceptance and approval from other people or groups.

This process of breaking away can be quite scary and it often leads to feelings of self-consciousness and a fear of rejection.

You might compensate for this by doing whatever it takes to get people to like you. You might begin a lifelong search for someone to love you. You might even start displaying strong attention seeking behaviour.

In extreme cases, strong stage 4 emotional needs can either trigger an obsession with being 'perfect' or lead to episodes of self-harming behaviour.

The true purpose of stage 4 is to go through all this and become secure enough in your own skin, to establish a solid identity as a unique individual.

Hopefully your parents will pull off the balancing act of allowing you the space to do this and the love, support, guidance and boundaries we all need if we're going to stay safe and healthy.

Assuming this is the case you'll naturally begin to move on to the next stage.

But how would you know if an adult was displaying insecure stage 4 behaviour?

You might notice they get anxious or show a lot of self-doubt. They might well try and distract you from seeing this by:

- Excessive 'people pleasing'.

- Boasting or exaggerating.

- Hiding behind designer labels.

- Wearing attention seeking tattoos, body piercings or extremes of fashion.

- Being seen at the latest 'in' place or being part of the 'in' crowd.

- Always looking for perfection and to over achieve.

- Moving from one relationship to the next searching for someone to love them.

- Dressing inappropriately for their age.

You could also see people driven to:

- Win awards.

- Be famous.

- Get rich.

All of this behaviour has its root in looking for a sense of identity and a feeling of security.

Do you know people who behave like this?

How well do you think your salon would perform if your behaviour was guided by stage 4 insecurity?

- How would it perform if you thought getting people to like you was the key?

- How would it perform if your behaviour was driven by anxiety or attention seeking?

- How would it perform if your focus was constantly on looking for love, wealth, fame, celebrity or perfection?

You can see the problems stage 4 insecurity could cause, can't you!

So to summarise: At stage 4 you're on a quest to discover who you are.

Now let's look at ...

STAGE 5: THE 'ROLE JUGGLING' STAGE

This is where the solid identity you've established as a unique individual helps you to live a balanced life with clearly identified roles to play.

By now you're capable of mature relationships that aren't driven by the underlying need for love and approval. You're able to reveal more of yourself to others without fearing their judgement or rejection.

You're more comfortable in your own skin, more accepting of others and you no longer expect your partner, friends or children to be perfect ... **or a clone of you.**

You understand that life isn't all about self-gratification. That chores need to be done and taxes need to be paid.

Your *ultimate goal* at stage 5 is to be happy, content and comfortable which sounds perfect but the 'inner you' can get a bit lost, so you solve this problem by identifying with the roles adult life brings, like being a:

- Parent.
- Spouse.
- Carer.
- Bread winner.
- 'Professional'.
- Entrepreneur.
- Lover.
- Friend or mate.
- Athlete.
- Artist.

These are just a few of the roles you might identify with *(think of them like labels)* and obviously becoming a Stylist/Therapist or Salon Owner could be seen as a label as well!

The purpose of work in stage 5 is to generate the income to pay for the lifestyle you want, without asking too much from you in return.

This means it's important that your work is compatible with your other roles and what you do will take account of issues like:

- The hours you have to work.

- How much you can earn.

- The length of time it takes you to get to and from work.

- Your ability to take time off if you need it or be free for the school holidays.

These may be some of the reasons why you own a salon and as a stage 5 adult you turn up, do what you need to do, take the money and go home to where 'life' really happens.

If you're at this stage, running your salon is not an essential part of your soul, it's not your life purpose or calling, it's just what you do to pay the bills.

This can still cause a **'Satnav'** software insecurity problem!

How?

Because research has shown that many of us have a deep inner need for meaning in what we do for a living.

You'd think that owning your own business would give you enough meaning, wouldn't you and in the beginning for most of us it does ... **but a surprising number of salon owners fall out of love with their salons for a reason we'll look at a bit later.**

If this is how you feel, you'll probably agree you need the 'SECURITY' your salon gives you in terms of money and a role ... but it doesn't scratch your emotional itch anymore and the truth is you'd rather be doing something else.

We'd be fools to think our staff and clients don't sense our lack of involvement!

Keeping our salon for the sake of security is bad enough ... *but sadly it can get even worse!*

As we know from the survey we looked at earlier, quite a high percentage of salon owners have businesses that aren't even bringing in the money needed to live the lifestyle you want. This means your 'SURVIVAL' in your roles as a parent, a partner, a provider or carer is under constant threat.

The fact you're not doing what you really want to do AND you're not making enough money can lead to real feelings of stress, resentment or helplessness as you desperately want to break free ... **but as you've probably noticed when you're stuck in 'The Survival Trap', whatever you try to do to break out doesn't seem to work!**

So reaching stage 5 isn't the answer to creating a successful salon either, because your virus can still cause you problems despite the fact you're now a mature adult.

So what is the answer?

How can you break away from the problems created by your insecurity virus infected software?

It's actually very simple.

Before we explain, let's just have a quick recap.

In **Stage 1** you wanted someone else to look after you and take responsibility.

In adult life you're sometimes comfortable taking responsibility and sometimes you're not.

Who decides ... you or your virus?

You know you have to take responsibility for what happens if life ... **your virus isn't so sure and when it's in control you'll try and feel better by finding ways to avoid taking responsibility if you can.**

In **Stage 2** you took what you wanted from others with no regard for the cost or consequences.

In adult life you're sometimes comfortable accepting you can't have what you want and sometimes you're not.

Who decides ... you or your virus?

You know you can't have what you want all the time ... **your virus isn't so sure and when it's in control you'll try and find ways to manipulate people or situations so you do get what you want.**

In **Stage 3** your sense of identity or security came from 'fitting in' and obeying other peoples rules.

In adult life you're sometimes comfortable fitting in with other peoples rules and sometimes you're not.

Who decides ... you or your virus?

You know you have to create your own rules for life, you also know you have to accept the need to cooperate with other peoples rules ... **your virus isn't so sure and when it's in control you'll try and feel better by creating a world where <u>your</u> rules apply, or by giving control of your life to someone else's rules.**

In **Stage 4** your sense of identity and security came from what other people thought of you.

In adult life you're sometimes comfortable with how other people feel about you and sometimes you're not.

Who decides ... you or your virus?

You know you can't control other peoples thoughts about you ... *your virus isn't so sure and when it's in control you'll try to find ways to manipulate how other people feel about you, so you can feel better about yourself.*

In **Stage 5** your sense of identity and security came from the roles you played.

In adult life you're sometimes comfortable with the roles life asks of you and sometimes you want more.

Who decides ... you or your virus?

You know there's more to you and your life than the roles you play ... *your virus isn't so sure and when it's in control it feels like the safest option is to stay in the role you're identified with, so it will sabotage any attempts you make to break out and do something new.*

Can you see that every step of the way through life your ability to grow and thrive has been at risk of being sabotaged by insecure thoughts?

Can you see that you'll **never ... NEVER ... NEVER** experience consistent long lasting emotional satisfaction if you try and run your salon using stage 1 to 5 behaviour ... **especially if your insecurity virus is still active!**

The good news is we can break out of the 1 to 5 trap.

All we need to do is neutralise your virus and move on to stages 6 and 7.

So let's deal with your virus first and then look at stages 6 and 7 in the next chapter.

Does that sound good?

Excellent ... then let's look at beating your virus!

For a start we'd recommend you take the time to read at least one extra book.

If you're a methodical person, like Julie for example, who works through a challenge from beginning to end, you'll enjoy taking a closer look at **'Stage Climbing'** by **Dr Michael Broder.** You'll enjoy it because it has a lot more detail about the stages than we've been able to share with you here ... **plus you'll learn some great step by step strategies for climbing out of each one.**

BUT!

Step by step isn't the only way to break free of stage 1 to 5 insecurity. There's another way.

This is good news.

Why?

Because many salon owners can't do methodical ... we're just not wired up that way, are we! Instead we trust our intuition or 'gut feelings' and if this is you, you're going to love this alternative approach.

Let's start with a fact ... the world we live on is shaped like a globe. It's a globe that spins in space as it orbits around the sun.

Can we agree on that?

We hope so, because it's in all the text books!

But hang on a second ... Imagine you're standing on your perfect beach, watching your perfect sunset unfold over a perfectly calm sea.

Imagine there's not a breath of wind in the air, the stunning colours of the sun as it sets are reflected by the sea, there's hardly a sound to be heard ... **just you and your perfect sunset sharing a perfect moment.**

As you're standing there, caught up in the wonder of this amazing natural event, you notice the earth appears to be flat, doesn't it ... **but it's just an illusion** and you know deep down inside it's really round.

The sun looks like it's moving as it sets in the sky, doesn't it ... **but it's just an illusion**, isn't it and your perfectly still beach is actually moving around the sun instead.

Why are we telling you this?

To make the point that the real world we live is in fact full of illusions, just like the one in this picture.

The thing is, once we get used to the fact that something's just an illusion the new reality stops being scary. In the 21st Century we accept the idea that the earth isn't flat, so we don't feel threatened by it. But did you know our ancestors did feel threatened and they persecuted great thinkers and scientists like **Copernicus** and **Galileo** when they dared to suggest the earth wasn't the centre of the universe!

In fact we could tell you many stories of great insights and discoveries like theirs, which created insecurity because they pointed towards illusions being treated as real.

It takes a while for a new truth to be finally accepted, but we're going to trust you understand the point we're making about life being full of illusions which seem real **'but we <u>know</u> are not'** and share with you the story of how Simon's 'insecurity virus' disappeared for ever when he understood another illusion he thought was real.

You won't be surprised to learn he reads many books, goes on a lot of courses and is very curious by nature.

For the last 20 years his main focus has been on discovering more about business, marketing and psychology so he could apply it to his passion for helping salon owners.

Psychology was important because he soon realised that understanding the way people think is the key to marketing and building successful businesses.

Simon instinctively understood that the ability to create trust, confidence and a sense of connection were important in every salon but 90% of the time something was stopping them from happening naturally.

In this book we've called that something ... **the insecurity virus.**

In his search for answers, Simon discovered many different tools and strategies for creating trust, confidence and connection, but the most effective ones appeared to be ...

- Positive thinking.
- Neuro Linguistic Programming (NLP).
- Cognitive Behavioural Therapy (CBT).
- Hypnosis.
- Meditation.

They all helped in different ways, but the results were never as easy or consistent as they promised to be and he knew instinctively that something was missing.

So the search continued.

More books, more courses...**he felt the answer was always just around the corner.** Then one day he was introduced to something so simple it couldn't possibly be what he was looking for, but as you've probably guessed ... **it was.**

All it took was a simple perspective change.

One minute the earth is flat ... the next minute you KNOW deep down inside it's just an illusion in spite of how it appears.

You just know.

Simon was introduced to this perspective change by speaker and author **Jamie Smart.** He heard Jamie explain how your brain creates your reality using 3 *principles* that underpin the nature of thought.

To help his audience understand the principles Jamie posed 3 simple questions which we'll ask you here.

These are not trick questions. The answers **are** the obvious ones ... but please answer them anyway.

1. Are you alive?
2. Are you aware you're alive?
3. Are you aware that you can think?

We told you the answers would be obvious, didn't we!

Of course you're aware you're alive ... **and to be aware you have to be able to think about it.**

In other words you only know you're alive and conscious because you can think, which means you create your whole reality with your thoughts.

There is no other way.

After listening to everything, Simon thought he could sum up what Jamie was pointing to as ... ***"Your thinking creates your reality, so it must create your feelings of insecurity. There is no other way. It might feel like insecurity comes from being judged, rejected, worried about money, your appearance or a thousand other things, but that's the illusion and it's all you have to understand."***

Intellectually this didn't seem like anything new, but he did have a nagging feeling he was missing something obvious, so as he often does, he was lying in bed one morning mulling everything over ... **when it happened!**

He saw the illusion Jamie was pointing to and suddenly all the important bits of knowledge about beating the insecurity virus he'd collected over the years joined up to make a complete picture, in a way they never had before and in that moment ... **his virus disappeared for ever!**

Because it happened so easily it took him a day or two to trust the fact it simply didn't exist anymore. He was suspicious because he'd spent so long learning how to control and beat the virus that the idea it was just an illusion took some adjusting to.

It took a while to accept it wasn't lurking in the background waiting to cause trouble if he gave it the chance.

But the truth is this ... **the second he 'KNEW' with a deep almost unconscious certainty the virus <u>was</u> just an illusion his brain stopped creating it.**

The illusion was replaced by the absolute knowledge that there's nothing to do except understand how you create your own amazing three dimensional, surround sound, version of reality **INSIDE** your head and it's **ALL** generated by your thoughts brought to life and made to seem real by the emotions and feelings you experience which means *life is an inside job ... it only has the meaning <u>you</u> give it.*

Accept the truth of this and it's only a small step to accepting insecurity can't be caused by external events or the behaviour of anyone **OUTSIDE** you.

It might look and feel like it can but that's ... **the 'Outside In' illusion.**

Here's a simple exercise that might, *just might*, help you get a glimpse of what we're pointing to.

Can we agree that when we think about ourselves we often use the phrase I am ... and then add a label to describe how we're feeling, what we're doing, or who we think we are.

For example:

- I am ... a salon owner.
- I am ... a mother.
- I am ... a therapist.
- I am ... depressed.
- I am ... rich.
- I am ... unhappy.
- I am ... lazy.
- I am ... honest.
- I am ... stupid.
- I am ... a procrastinator.

With that understood let's do the ... *I AM exercise.*

Below you'll see we've written **I am** ... 10 times. We want you to complete 10 I am statements you feel are true about yourself.

No one else is going to see your list, so be honest because it will be interesting for you to see what you think.

So here we go:

1. I am ...

2. I am ...

3. I am ...

4. I am ...

5. I am ...

6. I am ...

7. I am ...

8. I am ...

9. I am ...

10. I am ...

So how did you find that exercise? Was it easy or difficult?

It's surprising what our minds can come up, isn't it. Some people discover labels they didn't even know they believed about themselves!

Anyway, whatever you wrote was important and personal to you, but it doesn't change the fact that once you understand the 3 principles there's only one label ANY of us can truly give to ourselves which is this.

I AM.

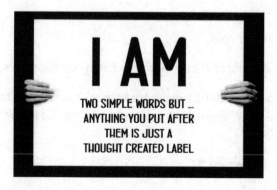

That's it ... *I AM!*

I AM is simply a statement that you exist and we agreed earlier, if you're alive, conscious and can think ... ***then you exist.***

Anything else you add after that, you're just using to define who you are, what you do, or how you feel and these are thought created labels.

<u>Here's the important point.</u> There's nothing wrong with thought created labels. It's how we as humans make sense of the world and keep ourselves sane.

The problem comes when we allow unhelpful labels like I AM ... NOT CONFIDENT to define us.

We treat them as real.

<u>**This**</u> is when we need to see we're living in a thought generated illusion ... **so we can let unhelpful labels go, when it makes sense to do so.**

Will Smith, in the film *After Earth* summed this lesson up beautifully when he was talking about fear to his frightened son.

He said:

"Fear is not real."

"The only place it can ever exist is in our thoughts."

"It is a product of our imagination, causing us to fear things that do not at present ... and may not ever, exist."

"This is insanity."

"Do not misunderstand me my son... danger is very real, but fear is a choice and we are all telling ourselves a story."

"The day I realised that ... my life changed."

We couldn't have put it better ourselves and if or when you're ready to see the illusion ... **your life can change as well.**

By the way you might like to know Simons experience isn't uncommon. Hundreds of thousands of people in countries all over the world are discovering the implications of seeing the 'outside in' illusion and word is spreading fast.

If you want to know more, we'd recommend reading **'*The Inside Out Revolution'*** by **Michael Neill** or **Jamie Smarts** latest book called *Clarity.*

Both are very easy to read and go much deeper than we've had time or space to do here.

All the books we've recommended so far are well worth reading but the blunt truth is, reading any book *(including this one)* will only give you knowledge, so now would be a good time to remind you of something you may have heard Julie say ...

Knowledge is power ... <u>but only if you use it!</u>

If you do use the knowledge we've shared with you in this chapter, to get some insights into your behaviour and finally see your insecurity virus for what it is, you'll find answering your big WHY questions in the next chapter very much easier!

Chapter 3

Answering Your Big **Why** Questions!

In this chapter we promised to complete the **7 Stages of Emotional Development** so let's have a look at ...

Stage 6: the 'Revealing Your Passion' stage

This is where you'll begin to find real, genuine, long term connection, happiness and fulfilment from your business.

Let's begin by agreeing that running a salon involves many responsibilities, here's just a small list to get us going:

- Marketing.
- P/R.
- Stock Control.
- Accounts.
- Wages.
- General admin.
- Health and safety.
- Staff recruitment.
- Staff training.
- Staff management.

- Staff leadership and motivation.

- Artistic or technical leadership.

- Customer service.

- Property maintenance.

- Strategic planning.

You can see they're all important parts of your business, can't you and as you're the salon owner it's obvious who is responsible for making sure they're done properly.

Of course you're responsible ... **but it doesn't mean you have to do them all yourself and hopefully by now you know it's a mistake to even try.**

So, if you're not driving yourself mad trying to do everything and be everything for your business, what should you be concentrating on?

The *first step* to answering this very important question is a simple exercise.

Get yourself a pen and paper. Find a quiet place where you can relax, safe in the knowledge you won't be disturbed, then just think back over your life and career.

We want you to make a list of everything you've EVER really enjoyed doing or felt passionate about.

Filter out the negative memories, just put a smile on your face and focus on remembering the good bits, the satisfying bits, the rewarding bits, the bits where you felt truly alive.

Focus on rediscovering everything that's ever given you a sense of feeling complete or whole and make a list.

When you've finished, give yourself a pat on the back, put your list down and leave it for 24 hours.

Then when you've given your mind time to settle, go back and add any other thoughts you've had.

Now your list is complete, you can look carefully at what you've written and we want you to look behind the words to discover the deeper reasons WHY you found these things so enjoyable.

When you look beyond the obvious what can you see?

Have you discovered that you feel most passionate and inspired ...

- When you can be creative?

- When you can be of service?

- When you feel a sense of achievement?

- When you help someone else to feel good about themself?

- When you feel everything's organised and under control?

This isn't a full list by any means so feel free to add your own ideas about what truly makes you feel whole.

By the way, if you honestly can't think of anything, then you need to get out of the salon owning business and you need to get out fast!

What's more likely is, you've remembered there **are** things you feel passionate about or inspired by and you'd love them to be in your life more of the time.

What stops this from happening?

Probably the fact you're being swamped by all the other stuff you believe comes with the role of salon owner and you don't know how to get it done for you.

If this is the case then you can relax because you'll begin to see how to change this as you go through the book!

For now we want you to imagine you've already reorganised your salon so it's become a true expression of your passion and you're in love with it ... **perhaps for the first time.**

It feels brilliant, doesn't it and it begs the question, what could be better?

Well, the answer to that lies in ...

Stage 7: Your 'Ultimate Purpose' stage

Now if you ever read the book *Stage Climbing* this is where you'll notice we've developed Dr Broder's ideas a bit.

In the book he talks of stage 7 as the stage where you're happy to give.

We agree ... but with a twist.

To us stage 7 is where things get really powerful because, *having got your own emotional needs met by discovering or rediscovering your passion in stage 6*, you're now at the stage where you're happy to give your team and customers all the help they need do the same.

You do it by giving them something to believe in and feel passionate about.

Your inspiring story!

It needs to be inspiring for a simple reason. When the story of the big WHY of your business connects with your staff and customers ... **everything changes.**

Why?

Well, once they feel the connection a decision is made deep down inside by the limbic part of their brains, **that your business feels like it's theirs!**

It feels like it's theirs because of the connection and they want to trust it. Actually it's more than that. It's because of how they feel that they want it to grow and be successful...which means they'll invest energy and commitment and they'll do it because they can't help themselves.

We *(both Julie and Simon)* know what this feels like.

It's what happened in our salons and it's the main reason we ended up as stage 7 salon owners and it all started with our own answers to the big WHY questions.

In other words we both had an inspiring story that was based on our passion and purpose.

That's right; we both created and ran our salons ... **on PURPOSE.**

So ask yourself ...

Do you know the answers to your big WHY questions yet?

Do you know what you're passionate about?

Do you know what the purpose of your salon is?

Do you have a promise you can make your customers?

Do you have an inspiring story to tell?

Probably not YET ... but you will soon!

LOCATING YOUR SALON STORY

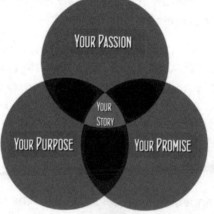

YOUR PASSION

YOUR STORY

YOUR PURPOSE   YOUR PROMISE

You will soon, because we'd like to help you see things more clearly by sharing some inspiring real life stories from other salon owners and hopefully this will help.

Let's start with Julies.

You may remember from our introduction that she's had to cope with quite a few personal challenges in her life.

As a child she was often told she wasn't good enough. An experience like that will either cripple you or make you stronger.

It made Julie stronger.

When she opened her first salon she knew she had a passion for great customer service and she was determined to create the best in her town.

Not just to prove that she **was** good enough in spite of everything. This would have been understandable, but it was more than that.

She knew what it was like to be unfairly judged and she was determined to create a salon where customers were attracted, **COMPELLED** in fact, to come back time and time again, because they felt so welcome and so comfortable.

Julie **NEVER** wanted her clients to feel unfairly judged like she'd done as she was growing up ... she wanted them to know they were accepted and OK.

This was her answer to the "Why does my salon exist?" question.

She also knew instinctively that, if she could pull it off, she would create a salon which was so special that customers and staff would feel attracted to it, inspired by it, stay loyal to it and become raving fans of it.

She realised she needed a story to make it come alive, so her staff and customers would feel the connection and her story was beautifully simple ... **the story of her business was built on her customer promise.**

The promise was this ... **_"We always make sure every customer feels like a welcome guest."_**

Making a promise an important part of your story is such a beautifully simple idea, because it immediately tells your customers what they can expect and your staff what they have to deliver and live up to.

Can you do the same?

Can you build on your passion to create a purpose that feeds a simple promise that resonates with people? A promise with a story at the heart of it so it comes alive and connects powerfully in a way that invites staff and customers to be part of it?

The chances are you can and we strongly recommend you do.

By the way we want you to notice specific words like **'always'** and **'every'** which Julie chose to use in her promise. They're powerful because they make it feel present, specific and alive.

It's not a bland, jargon filled cliché of a promise, is it. Instead it's like a Ronseal promise ... **_"it does exactly what it says on the tin!"_**

What about Simon?

Do you remember we told you that the first 5 years of his salon owning career were not happy? Do you remember him reaching his **SOD IT** point with all the typical salon owning problems he was constantly having to deal with?

That moment of emotion sparked a thought in his head that created an incredibly powerful WHY and the thought was ... *"I've got to find a way of making this business work properly whether I'm here or not!"*

He didn't realise it at the time, but until that moment of emotional discovery he wasn't being true to himself. He had a famous hairdressing father who cast a big shadow and he was driven to run his own salon like his fathers.

The blunt truth is they are very different people and it just wasn't working.

Simon's passion is helping people to help themselves.

He decided in that now famous **SOD IT** moment that the secret to creating a salon that would work whether he was there or not was to make his salon about his staff ... **not him!**

He understood he couldn't find the 'mini ME' clones of himself he'd been looking for until then *(and you'd be amazed how many salon owners desperately search for 'mini ME's' thinking that's the answer to all their problems)* but he <u>could</u> find lots of decent hard working staff who were desperately searching for an employer to give them more than just a job.

They were looking for an employer to inspire them and give them something bigger than themselves to believe in and belong to **and the obvious answer was, a team.**

Once he'd had the idea it took a while to bring the promise of **'a powerful self-managing team'** to life in a story and tell it in a way that connected, but as soon as it happened and his staff truly felt like they belonged, the way they felt about their customers changed, the quality of service changed, the level of connection changed.

Everything changed.

Can you see now why Simon's salon grew when he wasn't there for 6 months?

They didn't do it for him ... they did it for themselves.

Next, let's meet another salon owner, **Billy Mann** and we'll let Billy share how he discovered his story and promise.

Billy says:

"I'm a salon owner just like you and I live in the Southwest of Ireland where I grew up as part of a typical large Irish small town family."

"My family members were all in business, dealing with people every day, so it seemed inevitable that one day I'd be doing the same."

"By chance I fell into hairdressing and fell in love with it. After training in Ireland I was lucky enough to go to London for a while, which really opened my eyes to what I had to offer. Eventually I grew confident enough to return to my home town and open a salon."

*"At this time in my life it seemed like everything was going to plan but as you probably know yourself ... **things don't always go the way you expect!**"*

*"I got the salon up and running, assuming, because I came from a business background it would all be a piece of cake but ... **nothing could have been further from the truth.**"*

Because I'm good at what I do I quickly got busy and the logical next step was to recruit some good staff, but I struggled to find the right people. The staff I did manage to recruit were never consistently busy. Because of this I carried the salon for years and the blunt truth is ... I was the salon."

"No me no business."

"I felt like I was on a hamster wheel, working, working, working, carrying the staff and paying the bills. While this was going on my wife and I were busy raising a family of three children which created its own relentless pressure to provide. Finally it all got too much and the passion went from what I used to love to do."

"Owning my salon and doing hair wasn't enough anymore but the problem was I couldn't afford to leave. The only thing that made the situation bearable was the people I got to serve every day."

"I love people."

"I have no doubt that many of you reading this find yourselves in the same boat now. It's disheartening, tiring, frustrating and running your salon shouldn't feel like this."

"I've known Simon for a number of years and a few months ago I also experienced the perspective change he was describing in the last chapter and as my insecurities dropped away it had a profound effect on my ability to be happy."

"This finally gave me the freedom and courage to ask and answer the big WHY questions, which I had been avoiding up until then."

"I suddenly realised I'd been so busy doing the "What" of hairdressing and salon owning that I'd never stopped to ask myself "Why" I was in business at all."

"As far as I was concerned, it was about doing hair and earning a living."

"The answers to the WHY questions are obvious now, but I had so taken my gift of connecting with people for granted that I hadn't realised how special and important it was to me and my clients."

"The truth is I love helping people connect with themselves and the salon was a great way of doing that. I've had clients I've looked after for 20 years and I hadn't recognised that it was the deep connection to them and how I had helped them feel about themselves that kept us together ... It wasn't about their hair. That was just the excuse!"

"I also suddenly realised I didn't feel trapped anymore ... in fact I was in the ideal place."

"I now have a story ... the story of connection. At its core is **'the promise of the power of connection to change how we feel'**. Now I'm telling the story consistently my staff and customers are connecting with themselves and the salon in a whole new way."

"I've also become a 'Life Coach' and you won't be surprised to know most of my customers first come for a haircut!"

Can you see how what we've been talking about has changed everything for Billy?

Finally we'd like to introduce you to **Patrick Gildea.**

Patrick is based in Letterkenny in Ireland. If you'd seen him as a teenager you'd have been in no doubt that he was passionate about fashion and when he discovered hairdressing, it was a match made in Heaven.

Patrick stood out for another reason. From the age of 12 he was also very focused on earning money and he turned his hand to any work or business opportunity he saw potential in.

Is it any surprise that he opened his first salon at a fairly young age?

Not really.

Is it a surprise that his salon, which exuded his passion for delivering a high standard of service and hairdressing at surprisingly affordable prices, was a success?

Again ... not really!

It's fair to say that when the Irish economy took off in 1995 it gave a natural entrepreneur like Patrick a real opportunity to grow and prosper with it ... and he did.

At the peak of the boom he had seven salons but when the Global meltdown ripped the heart out of the Irish economy he came down to earth with a bump, insecurity kicked in and survival became his main focus.

This is understandable, but it also meant he fell into the **'The Survival Trap'** we mentioned in Stage 5 if you remember.

When you're in the trap it looks like the answer to your problems and the secret to getting out is generating as much turnover as you can ... but this is the illusion that set's the survival trap!

We've both noticed, time after time that the salon owners we meet who are stuck in the survival trap chasing turnover for its own sake, have either forgotten their WHY or they've never had one.

Patrick definitely had one, but he's a classic example of someone who forgot it for a while because of the illusion of recession created insecurity.

But not anymore!

It might have taken a few years, but once he saw what was happening and understood the price he was paying for chasing the turnover illusion, he very quickly took decisive action.

He did everything we are sharing with you.

He remembered his passion which revived his purpose and reminded him of his promise. He turned everything he'd **always** done - *but had taken for granted because he'd always done it* - into a customer story which he now shares wherever and whenever he can.

In just a few months, the difference his clarity has made is profound and we want to share Patrick's customer story with you, so you can see the power of passion, purpose and a promise brought together into a clear message for yourself.

Here it is.

*"When you choose the **Patrick Gildea Hairdressing Team** to look after you, you're choosing a group of people who are passionate about giving you the highest standard of hairdressing you'll find in the North West of Ireland."*

*"This passion has built a national reputation for offering a fantastic **Colour Correction Service** and **On Trend Colour Techniques.** This means if you want to add colour to your individually designed, precision haircut, you couldn't be in safer hands."*

*"This is because the foundation of everything the whole team offers you is an **'In Depth Consultation'.**"*

"This is an incredible experience because we know how to ask questions that get to the heart of what you really want and listen very carefully to what you have to say."

"The confidence and connection this creates between you and your stylist has to be experienced to be believed!"

"Our 'In Depth Consultations' are so special you need to make an appointment to get one!"

*"We know they work because clients often tell US how Colour brings their cut alive AND changes how they feel about themselves. We hear comments like **"It's taken years off me"** or **"I feel like me again"** all the time!"*

"The reason why you experience feelings like these when you embrace colour in your hair is simple. We combine the knowledge we gain from listening to you with our advanced colour products and techniques to create a unique individual result that truly is an expression of you."

"Even if you have sensitive skin we can look after you by using the kindest Organic Colour on the market. This contains natural ingredients like orange peel and banana and with its conditioning oil base and beautiful scent this ammonia free formula leaves your hair and skin feeling amazing."

*"Underpinning our reputation as colour experts is our education structure. Every single one of our stylists is a certified **Master Colour Technician** (MCT). This qualification is recognised as one of the industry's most prestigious awards and the Patrick Gildea Hair Dressing Team are the only people who can offer you the security of this level of education in the North West of Ireland."*

"Colour may bring your cut alive, but only if you've got the right cut for your head shape, bone structure and hair texture in the first place!"

*"By now you won't be surprised to learn that we take as much time and care educating our stylists as **Masters Cutters** as we do giving you world class colouring."*

"This means we can give every haircut a signature which is our way of saying your cut will always be created for you as an individual."

"We can do crafted cuts, sculpted cuts, classic cuts, timeless cuts, cheeky or elegantly understated cuts and your 'In Depth Consultation' guarantees you'll enjoy a haircut that compliments your face shape, your personality and your lifestyle."

"What more could you want to make you feel special!"

*"Our promise to you is simple. **From the moment we welcome you, your experience will be perfect.**"*

"A perfect experience could mean many things of course, but to us it stands for seeing you as a unique individual, taking the time to understand who you are and what you want, then making sure you get it."

"Delivering on our promise is something we take seriously, so we do more than train and reward great hairdressing skills, we continuously train and reward great customer service as well."

*"This all adds up to a team who are passionate about serving you ... **and it shows!"***

So now you've heard from four very different salon owners and we'd like you to ask yourself: *"What have I learned?"*

Did you learn from their passion, their early experiences in life and what came naturally to them?

We hope the answer is yes!

Were their stories and the promises that came out of them a natural extension of their passion turned into a way of serving others?

Yes again.

So this is a clue. You may not think you have a passion that makes you special or unique ... **but of course you have.**

Clues to what it is will be littering your past if you look for them and see them for what they are.

You're probably taking whatever **IT** is you're passionate about for granted simply because you've grown up with **IT** and **IT** seems normal to you.

Please don't make the mistake of taking your IT for granted ... instead look for the clues.

You'll often find them in what other people said to you, or what they were prepared to do for you. Look back to when people encouraged you, supported you, trusted you, responded to you and the clues to your powerful, life defining **IT** will be there.

Once you understand and own the passion that drives you and makes you special, you can use **IT** as your foundation to project your life forward in a way that serves others.

This becomes your purpose ... **and your purpose gives you the foundation of your story and the promise you build it on.**

Have we done enough to get you thinking with more clarity about your 3 Ps?

- Your Passion.

- Your Purpose.

- Your Promise.

Do you now understand why a story built around your passion, your purpose and your promise can create the foundation of a very different salon for you?

We hope so, but we accept that climbing step 1 of **'The 3 BIG Steps'™** is the most challenging.

It may be challenging but successfully climbing step 1 is the difference that makes the difference between owning a salon that works for you... and a salon that's just **HARD WORK!**

We also accept that there's a limit to what we can achieve to help you in a book.

If you can see what we're getting at but you know you need some practical help uncovering your IT, revealing your purpose, understanding your story and the promise you can make at the heart of it, you'll be pleased to know we've created a course called '**Climbing Big Step 1 ... Revealing Your WHY.'**

If you're interested you can find all the details by going to www.3bigsteps.com

CHAPTER 4

YOU CAN'T DO IT ON YOUR OWN!

If you remember we started our introduction to **'The 3 BIG Steps'™** comparing the process of creating a successful salon to completing a Jigsaw puzzle.

Most salon owners don't do Jigsaws for their own amusement but when we ask those who've got small children if they do them together, their answer is often yes!

When we ask how their child chooses a puzzle, it's always the one with their favourite character on the front. *Fireman Sam, Peppa Pig, Doc McStuffins, Postman Pat, Bob The Builder, Thomas the Tank Engine* ... it's the picture that lights children up because they link it with the feelings they get when they hear the stories.

This rather proves the case for having an emotionally attractive story and promise doesn't it!

But what about a strategy for putting their puzzle together ... do children bother about a HOW, or is it just a case of trial and error.

Their parents tell us that once they're old enough to understand, the HOW is important to children and they'll start with the corners or the edges or recognisable bits of their favourite character and work from there.

Well the same applies to you. There's no doubt you'll get your successful salon picture completed far more quickly if you've got a HOW strategy as well, so that's what climbing step 2 of **'The 3 BIG Steps'™** is all about.

The key principle to climbing to step 2 is ... YOU CAN'T DO IT ON YOUR OWN!

You can tell the story, you can provide passion and purpose as well, but you can't keep the promise ... **to do that consistently you need help.**

So what's your strategy for keeping your promise and how are you going to recognise attract and work with the right people to make it happen?

The first thing that can help you is the creation of some simple guidelines to act as a track for everything to run along.

If you remember Julie's promise is "We treat every customer like a welcome guest" and her guidelines are:

1. We welcome customers using their name.

2. We serve them as our guests while they are with us.

3. We make sure they feel special.

4. We invite them back again before they leave.

What would your simple guidelines look like?

Take a moment to jot down your thoughts right now if you can, while it's fresh in your mind.

Once you've got a story built on a customer promise and some guidelines you also need standards. You won't be surprised to know that Julies were ambitious. ***"Our promise has to be delivered 100% of the time to 100% of our customers by 100% of our team."***

Standards <u>are</u> important because to measure anything accurately you need something to compare it against.

You need standards of behaviour, standards of service and standards of performance so you can constantly measure your production to see what can be improved.

The standards have to come from you ... *it's your story after all*, but you can and should get your team involved in the **WHAT** of consistently delivering to your standards.

This normally involves creating systems which are essential if you're ever going to achieve **CONSISTENCY** and this is vital because without consistency there'll never be confidence, trust and connection and we know from the last chapter how important they are!

Putting all this together can seem a bit daunting but Julie came up with a concept that made the whole thing easy for her and her team.

She realised it helped everyone to think of your **HOW** like a theatre production.

When you do this, it puts the performance of your salon centre stage, right in the spotlight and makes things clearer, doesn't it.

In your theatre production:

- Your Salon Floor is the **Stage.**

- You're the **Director.**

- Your **Team** are your **Cast.**

- Your **Customers** are the **Audience.**

Can you see how simple all this is?

Just by changing the context of something we're all familiar with, *a stage production*, we've now got a much clearer picture of what needs doing and **HOW** we can bring some magic to getting everything done.

Obviously we've had the *'Your Salon Is A Stage'* conversation with quite a few salon owners over the years and one objection comes up time after time.

"If I give my staff a script to follow they'll seem wooden and lifeless and it won't connect with my customers."

We can see why you'd think that.

We've all experienced what it's like to be trapped by a sales person with zero charisma droning on through a sales script while we look for an excuse to escape, haven't we!

We've all seen actors performing on stage who've made us wince because they just weren't right for the part.

We've all heard singers singing in tune but completely missing the message of a song, so instead of moving us it leaves us cold.

When it doesn't connect, a performance is worse than useless, it's often very uncomfortable for the performer and the audience.

The good news is the answer to your natural concern is quite simple. If a good script or a powerful message isn't connecting ... it must be the performer.

Having a clear purpose and the customer promise that goes with it, guarantees you a good script and a powerful message, *this is why it's so important to know what yours is* and if it isn't connecting it's simply because the person you're asking to perform it doesn't **BUY the story of your WHY and isn't bothered whether they keep your customer promise or not!**

The connection between them and the role just isn't there. They don't believe it, they can't inhabit it. In other words you've cast the wrong person in the role and in the next chapter we're going to look at some simple ways to stop that happening!

Does this make sense?

In case you're still in any doubt this is the way to go, let's look at the alternative which is... **to let your staff communicate YOUR message THEIR way.**

What's wrong with that?

Because each staff member is different and how they feel changes every day, there will be no consistency to the delivery of **YOUR** message.

Consistency is essential... it's the magic ingredient!

We know a lack of consistency is a real issue because, *if you remember,* our survey showed **64%** of salon owners have problems getting their less experienced staff busy.

Why do less experienced staff struggle to get busy?

The reason is quite simple, it's our old enemy **INSECURITY**... and we looked at all the problems that causes in chapter 2!

Give the right cast members a role they believe in, good training and a powerful script or lyrics to deliver and you'll find insecurity drops away as if by magic, because they take confidence from being part of something bigger than themselves.

In other words by inviting someone who cares to be part of your cast you're giving them something to identify with and belong to... **identity and belonging are two powerful human needs.**

When they put the confidence of belonging on, like a coat you get what you really want ... **the consistent delivery of your customer promise.**

This is such an important point we hope and pray we're doing it justice and you can see what it means for you!

Assuming you can, you need to understand that the definition of a cast member who is 'right' to play a role in your performance is someone who is emotionally attracted to the same thing you are ... **and hopefully you're both attracted to serving the audience who are your customers.**

The audience come to your performance for their own reasons not yours **AND CERTAINLY NOT FOR YOUR CAST MEMBERS.**

They know what they want and we call it **CONNECTION.**

This means your cast members are not performing to please themselves, they're performing to give the audience what they want ... **and they want to feel like they belong, they want to feel like they matter, they want to feel like they've been noticed.**

We'll ask you again ... does this make sense?

Your job as the director is to provide a script packed with passion, purpose and a promise *(your story of course)* choose a cast who are inspired by it, create a set where everything can come together and direct all these elements create a performance that delivers a powerful connection with your audience ... **and do it consistently time after time.**

Remember it works because **emotion drives decision making behaviour, not logic.**

We use logic to rationalise emotional decisions **AFTER** we've made them. It's just the natural way our brains work.

In the context of our salons this means the long term, loyal raving fan clients every successful salon is built on, come for the connection ... **the haircut or the treatments you provide while you're connecting are just the logical excuse they need to justify coming to see you.**

It means, if you want loyal, long term, raving fan customers your production had better hit the connection spot consistently and basing your **HOW** on the concept of a performance is the way to do it.

Combine a great script, with the right set, clear directions and a talented cast and you'll find your salon production with its big WHY inspired customer promise, can wow your audience of loyal raving fan customers for years!

Chapter 5

Cast members who buy the story of your why!

If you're going to base your *How Strategy* on the performance of your cast then it begs the question **HOW** are you going to make sure you've got the right people in your cast?

Obviously you're looking for cast members who **BUY the story of your WHY** so they're motivated to deliver your customer promise consistently. Customers notice if you've got cast members who aren't motivated, don't they. If you're stuck with any you're going to have a tough time delivering a production that connects consistently with your audience.

With a lack of connection you'll get mixed reviews, poor word of mouth and before long the only way you'll be selling anything is by giving away your profits in the form of discounts and a constant stream of special offers!

This means it's essential to know who's going to make a great fit for your cast.

- Julie knows she needs people who don't judge others.

- Simon knows he needs people who want to be part of a team.

- Billy knows he needs people who want to connect.

- Patrick knows he needs people with a passion for fashion and high standards.

Can you see how much easier it is to identify the right people when you have a clear purpose and a customer promise to keep?

Now, do you already own a salon, or are you planning to open one?

If you're planning to open one and you don't employ anybody yet you can skip forward about 4 pages to the section on interviewing, because now we're going to look at how you can tell which members of the cast you've already got are right for you.

Here's a simple exercise that will show you. You'll need a piece of paper and a pen or pencil. When you're ready, make a list of the names of everyone you employ or who's involved in any way with helping you run your salon.

When you've done that, take each name on your list in turn, and based on your experience of working with them, ask yourself the following 4 questions one after the other. Don't stop until you get to the one you answer **YES** to, when that happens make a note of the question number.

(By the way make sure you go with your gut reaction when you're doing this exercise and take no more than 5 seconds to answer any of the questions.)

1. *Is this person a true 'believer' and do they have the skills I need to be right for my cast?*

YES or NO

If your answer is no, then move on to the next question.

2. *Is this person a true 'believer' but their skills need improving to be right for my cast?*

YES or NO

If your answer is no, move on to the next question.

3. *Is this person NOT a true 'believer' but has the skills needed to be right for my cast?*

YES or NO

If your answer is still no then move on to the final question and ask yourself.

4. *Is this person NOT a true 'believer' and their skills need improving to be right for my cast?*

YES or NO

If you've followed our directions and completed this exercise you should now have a list of names with a number from 1 to 4 next to each one.

Now before we look at what to do with your answers, just ask yourself, who deserves your time, energy, support and encouragement:

- The people who are **true believers** and passionate about keeping your promise consistently?

- Or the people who aren't and won't!

The answer is obvious isn't it! You work with those who are and will. They're the people who you said yes to in questions one or two.

Make sure you nurture, involve and appreciate your numbers ones.

Do the same for your number twos and add an intensive training program to elevate their skills.

Your threes and fours need to move on to different casts where they may be a better fit.

To make this happen without having to go down the disciplinary route ... *just do two things:*

1. Every time threes or fours breaks a rule or cause a problem, take them to one side and in a quiet, non-emotional, **professional** manner, tell them what they've done wrong, explain it's unacceptable, be very clear what the consequences will be if they do it again **and don't wimp out of delivering the promised consequences if they do cross the line!**

2. Every time they do something positive that you want to encourage, **pay them the compliment of noticing and saying well done.**

The rest of the time, don't try to **'motivate'** or **'change'** them. Simply **ignore** their behaviour except for the usual day to day need to be polite and work together ... put your energy and attention into the positive things that are happening in the salon.

Important Point!

Only someone who's got rid of their insecurity virus will be able to do this consistently, but if you do manage it, one of two things will happen very quickly:

1. *Your threes and fours will get fed up because their tactics aren't working anymore and leave.*

2. *Your threes and fours will modify their behaviour to get more of the praise they now deserve and you won't want them to leave!*

Either way your cast and performance just got better!

Remember, your threes and fours are not necessarily bad people they're just in the wrong cast!

Don't change your production to suit the people who don't **BUY the story of your WHY** ... instead help them move on in a professional way with dignity and maturity.

The reason why we say don't try and motivate or change your threes and fours is simple. **80% of the time you won't succeed** ... you'll just waste time and energy you could be putting into your ones and twos so their performance gets better and better!

We hope you agree ... because if there's one lesson we've seen too many salon owners learn the hard way, it's this.

A cast with even ONE member who doesn't BUY the story of your WHY and want to keep your promise, will unravel like a ball of string because the trust, confidence and connection between members just isn't there.

This means a salon owner who ignores this lesson and invests their time trying to turn the non-buyers round rather than working with those who buy naturally, will eventually lose their good cast members because of it.

Is that what you want?

Probably not, but we've seen it happen time after time ... so you have been warned!

Now let's look at recruiting new cast members and it's essential to have a structured, professional recruitment process in place.

To do this we're going to look a much improved version of the process Simon shared in his last book and the first thing we need to focus on is attracting the right candidates.

It all starts with an attractive advert.

To be attractive you need to know who you want to attract. We'd suggest:

- ✓ People who **BUY your WHY.**

- ✓ People who are already busy because it proves their ability to deliver.

- ✓ People who are fed up enough with their current situation that they're ready to move.

The secret is to create an advert that ...

- ✓ Allows them to see themselves.

- ✓ Allows them to see that you understand them and their problem.

✓ Allows them to see that you have the answers and they can trust you to deliver.

This means your advert needs to speak to the conversation they're having in their heads about what's frustrating them at work and then you can back up your ability to offer something different by explaining your big WHY.

So for example an advert that said ...

"IF YOU'RE AN EXPERIENCED STYLIST (OR THERAPIST) WHO'S FED UP WORKING IN A BITCHY ATMOSPHERE WE'VE GOT THE ANSWER!"

IT'S TRUE. THE WHOLE REPUTATION OF OUR BUSY SALON IS BUILT ON OUR PROMISE TO *(INSERT YOUR PROMISE HERE)* AND THE FACT WE'RE ALL PASSIONATE ABOUT KEEPING THIS PROMISE GUARANTEES AN INCREDIBLE ATMOSPHERE TO WORK IN.

WE ASK A LOT OF YOU AND WE GIVE YOU A LOT IN RETURN.

- WE PAY WELL.

- WE PROVIDE ONGOING MOTIVATION AND TRAINING.

- WE TREAT YOU WITH RESPECT.

WE TRULY BELIEVE YOU'RE LOOKING AT AN ADVERT FOR ONE OF THE BEST STYLIST (OR THERAPIST) JOBS IN *(INSERT YOUR REGION.)*

WE'D LOVE YOU TO TRUST ENOUGH TO FIND OUT MORE. PLEASE CALL *(INSERT NAME AND NUMBER).* THEY'LL BE HAPPY TO ANSWER ANY QUESTIONS YOU HAVE AND ORGANISE AN ABSOLUTELY CONFIDENTIAL INTERVIEW IF THAT'S WHAT YOU'D LIKE.

Can you see how an advert like this ticks all the boxes?

"Did You Notice That The Headline Had Capital Letters All The Way Through And Was Set In Inverted Commas?"

This is statistically proven to increase the number of people who will read it. You might also have noticed our personal preference is to screen applicants briefly on the phone, rather than asking for a CV or application form.

Why?

Because, we believe it's the cheapest and fastest way for you to sift out unsuitable candidates.

The fact is, talking to someone will tell you a lot more about what they're really like, than something they've written.

This is because research has shown that 40% of application forms and CVs sent in contain *shall we call them 'factual inaccuracies'* and even the truthful forms will have important facts left out and a positive gloss put on everything!

Now let's assume you've got some worthwhile **'applicants'** and move on to the selection process.

How do you create a selection process that helps you find out if a potential cast members truly does **BUY the story of your WHY?**

- You do it by building a clear picture of the self-image, beliefs, values and attitude of the person you're thinking of employing, **as quickly as possible.**

- You do it by not relying on **your** judgement alone. ***You get the people they're going to be working with involved in the decision as well.***

- You do it by not just relying on an interview and trade test to make your final decision. ***Your selection process should have several steps and take 3 months in total.***

Now we agree that a 3 month selection process might seem a very long time, but you'll see later on in the book just how much employing the wrong person can really cost you, so it's worth getting it right at the beginning, isn't it!

Before we get into detail about the **'process'** ... *here are two guiding principles to follow:*

1. **Don't be desperate:** *We truly believe it's better to have no staff than the wrong staff!*

2. **Don't take __anything__ you're told at face value:** *Use it as a starting point for further discussion and that's it!*

Follow these principles and you won't go far wrong.

When you interview, choose a suitable venue that sets the right tone. Don't use your staff room or anywhere you can be interrupted. If you don't have a suitable place in your salon, use a local hotel. We've held many interviews in hotel lounges and found as long as you buy tea or coffee at regular intervals they're quite happy for you to be there.

How and where you sit is important; so to help you get your body language right, sit at the same level as the person you're interviewing with no barriers between you and preferably at a 90 degree angle to them.

Remember, while you're interviewing, what you're **really** looking to discover is ... **do they BUY the story of your WHY?**

The secret to this is practicing 'quiet listening' which gives candidates space to open up and reveal who they are. Combine this with some simple questions and you'll discover that interviewing becomes **very** easy for you!

Calmness and quiet curiosity are the keys to getting your candidate to reveal themselves, so start by asking one of the interview questions we'll give you in a moment and settle down to listen.

Forget about watching like a hawk. Forget about copying their gestures. Forget about searching for the key words they say ... **in fact don't even think about what you're going to say next!**

Just stay calm, relaxed, keep regular eye contact, smile from time to time, be attentive and interested and when something they say makes you curious, just follow your instinct and ask more about that.

Don't forget, you've got **2** eyes, **2** ears and only **1** mouth, so as a guide you should aim to listen *at least four times as much as you talk!*

WARNING!

Don't get sucked in ... Instead, be prepared to leave space

for silence and when you do, your candidate will feel compelled to fill it and you'll be amazed at what comes out of their mouth.

If you find you're getting through the questions in less than half an hour it's a sign that you're not using 'quiet listening' effectively which means you're not giving your candidates room to reveal themselves to you.

If this happens, just practice until it becomes second nature. It won't take long!

With that point understood, here are the questions.

1. *"If I was talking to your best friend, what 3 words do you think they might use to sum up 3 different parts of your personality?"*

2. *"Sometimes we're inspired by people we know, sometimes it's someone we read or hear about. I'm interested to know who you think has been the most inspiring person in your life."*

3. *"Research has shown Stylists (or Therapists) enjoy their job more than many other professions ... what do you feel makes it so enjoyable?"*

4. *"If I gave you £500,000 and said you had to spend it all in the next 24hrs or give it back to me, what would you choose to do with it?"*

5. *"Everyone in our team needs to be comfortable taking responsibility so I'd like you to give me an example of something you've done that shows you're a responsible person."*

6. *"What does the word team mean to you?"*

7. *"If money was no object; what would you do on your perfect holiday?"*

8. *"Tell me about the last time you felt really successful."*

9. *"What do you feel is the most important quality or gift you'd bring with you if you join us!"*

10. *"What would be your favourite shape if you could choose from a squiggle, a square, a circle and a triangle? (Then ask for their second favourite etc)"*

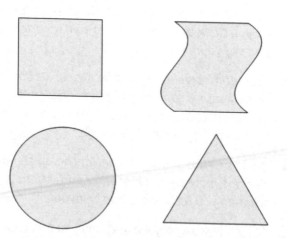

When they've chosen say ...

"The 'order' you put the shapes in normally reveals a lot about your key character traits. For example your selection suggests" and then you'd use the following guidelines to put together their profile.

A true square:

- Is well organised.
- Loves detail.
- Makes lists.
- Hates being late.
- Always tidies up and puts things away after they've finish using them.

A true circle:

- Is easy to be around.
- Enjoys entertaining them or looking after them.
- Is empathetic and a good listener.
- Only feels complete when they're in the company of other people.

A true squiggle:

- Loves change.
- Is flexible by nature.
- Often change their minds.
- Can be late disorganised and untidy.
- Is capable of coming up with great ideas.

A true triangle:

- Is driven to achieve.
- A clear communicator, direct and to the point.

- Is focussed and goal orientated.

- Is competitive.

- Is not always sensitive to the needs of the people around them.

The chances are you won't get a complete match, because most of us are a combination of at least two shapes, if not three and the exercise is only about 80% accurate.

The good news is, it doesn't matter if the result suggested by the test is right or wrong!

If it's right they'll be amazed. If it's wrong they'll tell you and you reply ... *"that happens sometimes because it's only 80% accurate, so tell me, what are you really like"* ... and the amazing thing is, because the exercise has given them a framework to compare themselves against, they'll tell you far more than if you'd just asked them without doing the shapes.

Once you think you've got a clear picture, it's time to check!

Doing this is fun and easy. Take the key trait or traits that have come to the surface and go exploring and don't be afraid to be a little provocative!

If it appears they are well organised you can ask ... **does that tend to drive the people around you nuts?**

They might laugh and agree with you, or they might get defensive, either way, you've learned something, so dig some more!

If it appears they're a great people person you can say ... **tell me about the last big argument you had with someone.**

Can you see how being a little provocative like this might reveal another side to your potential cast member?

You might like to know that when we first did the shapes exercise many years ago we found Simon was a Squiggle 1st and Triangle 2nd. However, Julie was a Triangle 1st and Squiggle 2nd so perhaps you can see why we complement each other so well!

Talking of working well, we suggest:

- You look for people who are a combination of squiggle and circle to look after customers with creative needs.

- You look for people who are a combination of circle and square to look after customers with more technical or process based needs.

- You be very wary of the triangle and square combinations if teamwork and cooperation are important, because they know exactly what they want and they're not afraid to tell anyone!

- You take note of the fact that the triangle is the symbol of the leader so you'll find it more often in salon owners than their staff. We find that triangles don't stay in the long term; they are driven to move on and find something better, or create it for themselves.

Now, let's go back again to the selection process. If after you've had your **'quiet listening'** chat you're pretty sure the person isn't who you're looking for, simply thank them for coming and tell them when and how you'll let them know about your decision.

If you do think they have potential, pay them the compliment of saying so, and then ask: *"What questions would you like to ask me?"*

As you answer their questions, look for the right time to give them a clear picture of what they can expect if they're successful.

This means telling making the story of **'WHY your business exists and the promise it's based on'** truly come alive.

It also means making it very clear that delivering your customer promise with passion and connection isn't just a **'when you feel like it'** option.

It means going through your guidelines as well.

As you're explaining these things and making them come alive, be prepared to ask them what they think.

When they tell you, be prepared to dig deeper with follow up questions like ... *"why do you say that"* and go back to using quiet listening so you can really draw them out.

When you've finished your interview you then have to decide if they're good enough to go on to the next stage of your hiring process.

If they are, this is where it pays to get the rest of your cast involved.

Depending on what the applicant is currently doing you have to be flexible with this next step, but we suggest you arrange for them to spend as much time as is practical in the salon, but ideally it would be a couple of days. While they are with you get them to contribute as much as they can to the running of the salon, including doing customers or models, cleaning, taking part in meetings and so on.

At the end of that time ask every member of your cast what their decision would be and if **any** of them say no, that's it ... the applicant goes no further. If they all say yes *(and normally they do)* then offer your applicant a 3 month trial.

By the way, if you find that one cast member often says no, it can be sign of insecurity and they could well be a number three or four ... and you know what that means!

At the end of the 3 month trial period, just ask your cast for their final decision and <u>again</u> if anyone says no ... the applicant leaves.

Now the reality is, if there are any doubts or problems they tend to surface much sooner than 3 months and if they do crop up you need to investigate and try and solve the problem ... once!

If it doesn't work take it as a sign and the applicant leaves.

And that's it.

You've come to the end of a powerful, widely used tried and tested recruitment process that can transform your salon. Also by involving your cast in the decision making process you've built trust with them in a very powerful way.

So that's how you find people who **BUY the story of your WHY** ... next we need to look at some guidelines on HOW to work with them!

CHAPTER 6

HOW TO BRING OUT THE BEST PERFORMANCE FROM YOUR CAST

Here's a bold statement.

The secret to being a great director is leadership ... <u>NOT MANAGEMENT!</u>

Most salon owners we ask don't seem to think there's a difference, but believe us when we say ... **the difference is huge!**

In its simplest form, leadership is about a people focus and management is about a process focus.

If you lead people well, they automatically create good, efficient, effective management processes as they work, simply because they want to ... not because they have to and this makes the huge difference we mentioned.

Leadership is about inspiring, motivating and growing people with the right vision, the right tools and the right behaviour and to make this point we'd love to share a great Walt Disney quote we heard while attending a training course held recently by *"The Disney Institute"* which goes like this:

"YOU CAN DESIGN CREATE AND BUILD THE MOST WONDERFUL PLACE IN THE WORLD BUT IT TAKES PEOPLE

TO MAKE THE DREAM COME TRUE."

We feel Walt is agreeing with us when we say ... ***"It's not what we do but the way we do it that makes the difference"***

Making the way that we do it ... the 'right' way takes leadership, of course and here are some of the things we've noticed great leaders do.

- ✓ Because they have a clear purpose they know what they stand for and what they want to achieve so they are able to communicate it clearly to cast members ... their cast aren't mind readers!

- ✓ They follow Ghandi's advice when he says '*Be the change you want to see*'... in other words they lead by example!

- ✓ They take responsibility for their business by **giving** responsibility to each individual for their performance within the business.

- ✓ They communicate regularly and consistently with their cast, so they can share their progress and give recognition where it's been earned.

- ✓ They're not afraid to set standards and strive for consistency using systems, because they allow you to measure performance and progress.

- ✓ They strive to create relationships that can last a lifetime with their customers and team members.

✓ They have the ability to spark enthusiasm and excitement in others by being prepared to be creative in how they communicate what they want others to do.

Hopefully, by now, you understand that leadership is a skill you personally need to develop, live and breathe if your cast is going to give the consistent performance they are truly capable of.

The concept of **'growing people'** which we both believe in so passionately is based on the ground breaking research of **Abraham Maslow** who developed the famous *Hierarchy of Needs* model in the USA in the 1940s and 1950s. Many years may have gone by since he created it, but Maslow's theory remains just as valid today for understanding human motivation and personal development at work.

Now as often happens when an idea gains many followers, like Maslow's did, they find different ways it can be applied … and we're no exception, so what we're about to share with you is unashamedly *'our salon version'* of the principles that were first taught all those years ago.

If any of your cast gets stuck at the bottom of the hierarchy you'll know, because they'll turn up, go through the motions and go home. That's it. As their employer and leader that's all you'll get and sadly it's **all** the majority of employers **ever** get from most of their staff!

If you've got a member of your cast who isn't interested in growing, the chances are they don't **BUY the story of your WHY** and you scored them as a three or four in the exercise we did earlier. If this is true and you haven't done it already, you need to be moving them on because as we said before, their attitude will kill your performance, if you don't!

If your cast members are prepared to go beyond just **'going through the motions'** it will be because you've done what's needed to create the trust, confidence and connection that allows them to grow.

This is why we've placed so much emphasis on leadership because it provides the right foundations for trust, confidence and connection.

When it comes to the right foundations, your behaviour has a big role to play. Do you remember Ghandi's quote from earlier about ***"Being the change you want to see"***?

Simon readily admits to having 13 bad habits he had to change before he could **'be the change he wanted to see'** in his salon and it took a lot of soul searching for him to accept this, but when he understood Maslow's principles and improved his leadership behaviour his team started to **BUY the story of his WHY** and the results were amazing.

Have a look for yourself now as we go through all 13 and discover whether any of **your** habits might be making it difficult for your team to **BUY the story of your WHY.**

HABIT NUMBER 1: BEING SELFISH

The little voice in your head might say ...

> *"It's my business. I'm the one who's taken the risks. I'm*

the one who's legally liable if things go wrong. I'm entitled to see things my way ... aren't I?"

A real leader would reply ...

"Not if you want your cast and clients to invest in you and your big WHY. You're asking them to care, commit and trust. Do you seriously think they'll do this if you're selfish? You have to accept you're in this together if you want to achieve any sort of long lasting success."

Habit Number 2: Having favourites

The little voice in your head might say ...

"Some people behave better than others, don't they? They work harder, earn me more money and cause me fewer problems, why shouldn't they be my favourites; it's only natural ... isn't it?"

A real leader would reply ...

"No!"

"Having favourites is normally a symptom of a cast with number three's and fours in it. The good news is, when they leave and the natural frustration you feel about their attitude and behaviour leaves with them, having favourites becomes an easy habit to drop!"

HABIT NUMBER 3: TALKING ABOUT PEOPLE BEHIND THEIR BACKS

The little voice in your head might say …

> *"Some people can be difficult, oversensitive, take things the wrong way, or never listen, so there's no point saying anything to them … at the same time their behaviour annoys the **** out of me, so I talk about it to people I trust and feel will understand. That's OK … isn't it?"*

A real leader would reply …

> *"Not really!"*

> *"Having members of your cast you don't feel comfortable talking to is just another symptom of your insecurity virus at work. It also means you've got threes and fours hiding in your cast so do something about it!"*

HABIT NUMBER 4: MAKING PROMISES TO YOUR STAFF THAT YOU DON'T KEEP

The little voice in your head might say …

> *"Running a salon isn't easy, there are bound to be times when I make promises I can't keep … right?"*

A real leader would reply …

> *"Think about it. Feeling stressed and having to*

engage in constant firefighting are classic signs of a disorganised salon owner with no purpose or customer promise. It's also a sign of a raging insecurity virus. Making promises you can't or don't intend to keep doesn't solve anything, it just puts the day when your salon will become a success even further into the future!"

HABIT NUMBER 5: BEING INTOLERANT, IMPATIENT OR HOLDING GRUDGES

The little voice in your head might say ...

"It's understandable if I get a bit grumpy, or sometimes hold a grudge against people who don't care about me, or do what I want ... isn't it?"

A real leader would reply ...

"You wouldn't trust a dog who licks your face one day and bites you the next ... why should anyone trust you if you're in the habit of doing the same? They won't and intolerance is just another sign of the insecurity virus at work."

HABIT NUMBER 6: BEING JUDGEMENTAL

The little voice in your head might say ...

"I know what I want. I know my problems would all disappear if only I could find more people who think like I do ... right?"

A real leader would reply ...

> *"Constantly judging people against your own standards and pointing out where they don't meet them is the habit that makes perfectionists impossible to work with. Trust us, it's not a sign of strength ... it's your insecurity virus again!"*

HABIT NUMBER 7: NAGGING AND BULLYING

The little voice in your head might say ...

> *"When it feels like cast members don't listen or care, I've got to show them I mean business by keeping on at them until they do ... right?"*

A real leader would reply ...

> *"Wrong!"*

> *"Behaviour like this is another classic sign of your insecurity virus doing what it does best. Destroying your ability to trust and build relationships. You know what to do about it by now, don't you ... you've got it, deal with that insecurity virus!"*

HABIT NUMBER 8: BLAMING OTHERS RATHER THAN SHARING OR TAKING RESPONSIBILITY

The little voice in your head might say ...

> *"When things go wrong because mistakes are being made it's only natural to make sure others take the*

blame. If I don't, they'll think I'm weak or incompetent ... right?"

A real leader would reply ...

"A strong leader understands that collective responsibility is a very powerful trust building tool and your cast will naturally weed out and deal with members (who'll be threes and fours of course) who make the same mistakes over and over again."

"But ... here's a great team building tip, when the s**t hits the fan the leader (you) should always be prepared to take responsibility for what's gone wrong. You'll be amazed at the trust this builds."

HABIT NUMBER 9: BEING INCONSISTENT OR UNFAIR WITH PRAISE AND DISCIPLINE

The little voice in your head might say ...

"It's normal to take good staff for granted, isn't it? They're causing no problems and taking good money, so surely I need to focus my attention on my problem people ... right?"

A real leader would reply ...

"Only if you want more problems!"

"What you focus on is what you get more of. Focus on the insecurity of the three and four type behaviour and you'll shine the light on your own insecurity and end up with more problem behaviour, not less! Is that what you really want ... we don't think so!"

HABIT NUMBER 10: NOT MEASURING PERFORMANCE OR GIVING FEEDBACK

The little voice in your head might say ...

> *"My business figures confuse me and if I tell my staff they need to do more they either agree but then nothing changes, or they make excuses instead. It's better to keep quiet ... right?"*

A real leader would reply ...

> **"Think about it. A jigsaw puzzle is satisfying because you can see your progress. A jigsaw puzzle keeps you involved because you can quickly tell if a piece doesn't fit and try something different. Your team need to feel satisfied and involved and they won't if they don't feel they are getting anywhere!"**

HABIT NUMBER 11: NOT TRUSTING

The little voice in your head might say ...

> *"It's normal not to trust everyone, isn't it! Nobody's perfect and human nature being what it is they're bound to take advantage if I don't watch out ... right?"*

A real leader would reply ...

> **"Lack of trust is just another symptom of your insecurity virus at work and the good news is once it's gone and you start trusting you'll find they watch your back for you ... so you don't have to!"**

HABIT NUMBER 12: NOT CONSULTING OR INVOLVING

The little voice in your head might say ...

> *"What's the point of asking their opinions? They either don't know, or don't care, so it's better to just get on with running the salon ... isn't it?"*

A real leader would reply ...

> **"Research has shown that being secure enough to let go and give cast members a degree of control over their environment and the decisions that affect them is one of the most powerfully connecting things you can do. Yes it can take a bit longer, but done right you end up with better decisions, more emotional engagement, higher levels of performance and you guessed it ... more trust!"**

And finally - you'll be relieved to know ...

HABIT NUMBER 13: NOT LISTENING

The little voice in your head might say ...

> *"Why do I need to go through the hassle of listening when all they do is moan, complain or make excuses, it's just a waste of time ... isn't it?"*

A real leader would reply ...

> **"Not at all!"**

> **"Why? Because all the research shows that being secure enough to let go of our own thoughts and**

practice 'quiet listening' instead is another powerful way to create meaningful connection with someone else. It means it's a brilliant way to build trust, confidence and connection when you're communicating with your cast."

"By the way we don't even need to have the answers, just giving people the opportunity to be heard without pressure or judgement gives them the space and permission to come up with their own answers ... and they always prefer those!"

These bad habits are all very human responses to the typical things that make a salon owners life a challenge, but a leader with a clear purpose who understands human nature and works with it, will find them all fading away.

You'll no doubt have noticed there were quite a few references to your insecurity virus and dealing with number threes and fours in our list of bad habits. We deliberately included this section because it helps you see the importance of what we were discussing in big Step 1 from another perspective.

The good news is when you get your cast members to the stage where they feel confident, trusted and connected with you, your story, your customer promise and their fellow cast members, you'll find them naturally taking responsibility for their performance.

This not only makes your salon a much nicer place for everyone to work in and customers to visit, it will also save you a lot of money!

Why?

Because staff turnover costs you money and a salon culture based on confidence, trust and connection creates loyalty ... **which saves you money.**

Your staff will stay loyal because they know they can't get what you're giving them anywhere else. Keep on being a great leader and you'll also find good staff from other salons ringing you up to ask for a job. You'll get to the stage where you're spoilt for choice!

As we said earlier if you lead well you don't have to spend most of your time **'managing'** your salon, your cast will do it for you and they'll do it because they want to.

But you need to understand that your job as a leader is to be the director ... **YOU MUST NEVER MAKE THE MISTAKE OF TRYING TO BE A MEMBER OF THE CAST AS WELL.**

You can be friendly, you can be professional ... **but you absolutely must be separate from your cast.**

Why is this so important?

Because if you're the leader AND a member of the cast, it doesn't matter how well you delegate responsibilities, you'll find your cast members delegating them back to you in the end ... **They see you as one of them so it's just what happens.**

Have we done enough to get you thinking with more clarity about HOW you can identify the right people to work with and how you can work with them in a way that engages them and releases the potential of your big WHY story and promise?

We hope so, but we accept that climbing **step 2** of **'The 3 BIG Steps'™** can also be challenging. It may be challenging but as we said earlier ... **YOU CAN'T DO IT ON YOUR OWN!**

It's also obvious that once again there's a limit to how much we can help you in a book ... so if you want more ... if you want some practical help uncovering your HOW strategy, assembling your cast and working with them effectively, you'll be pleased to know we've created a course called *'Climbing Step 2 ... Developing Your HOW.'*

You can find all the details by going to www.3bigsteps.com

CHAPTER 7

IT'S THE LITTLE THINGS THAT COUNT!

We're going to assume you've climbed big Step 1 and built your story around a promise. Let's also assume you've climbed Big STEP 2 and are clear about your strategy, your cast and how to be a great director.

WHAT'S NEXT?

Big STEP 3 of course.

The key principle for climbing big Step 3 is: It's the little things that count.

Before we get stuck into sharing the nuts and bolts of WHAT you need to be asking and organising to deliver the little things that add up to a big experience ... **we need to sound a word of warning.**

There's a danger you're going to feel much more comfortable with the WHAT material coming up and get sucked into focussing on it ... **instead of starting with WHY and HOW first.**

This would be a mistake.

'The 3 BIG Steps'™ are in the order they are for a reason ... **they work with human nature**. This means they allow you to combine the human spirit with an organised salon.

It would be a mistake to stick with:

- What you know.

- What's comfortable.
- What seems easier.

It would be a mistake that condemns you to many more wasted years, going round in circles, making very little progress.

Accepting this point, it's obvious you need effective systems and processes in place, to deliver your customer promise consistently.

You also need standards and measurement so you KNOW whether your customer promise is being delivered consistently.

A great director is not afraid to set standards ... Do you have clear standards and measurement at the moment?

WHAT should good BEHAVIOUR look, feel and sound like in your salon?

Your cast members need to know WHAT you expect and WHAT the consequences are if they don't deliver, simply because:

- If you don't know what you want ... **they can't deliver.**
- If you don't train them ... **they can't deliver.**
- If you don't provide consistent consequences, both good and bad ... **they won't bother to deliver consistently, only when they feel like it.**

The same rules apply for good SERVICE so ask yourself ... WHAT should it look, feel and sound like in your salon?

You also need to ask yourself WHAT good PERFORMANCE should look, feel and sound like as well!

By the way we are often asked for help with performance standards and we are reluctant to be too prescriptive, *every business is different after all*, but here are some thoughts that might help.

Let's take profit.

Making a profit may not be the sole purpose of your business but for long term success and your ability to be of service it is essential.

So if you believe, as we do, that a salon should deliver 20% operating profit as a standard then you need to create other standards to underpin and deliver it.

This means creating budgeting standards.

Standards like ... we budget to spend:

- **5%** of turnover on rent or mortgage.

- **14%** of turnover on stock.

- **40%** of turnover on wages.

- **8%** of turnover on everything else.

This leaves us **13%** to pay the VAT man and **20%** profit.

Add the entire list of **%** up and you get to **100%** including your standard of **20%** profit.

If you spend more on rent, it means you've got less to spend on stock or wages.

It's your decision to make but to deliver your standard of 20% you MUST do what you need to do find cost effective ways of keeping your promise.

If you're convinced that extra turnover is essential then rather than chasing new clients with special offers, consider putting up your prices. If you feel you can't, then it means you and your cast haven't successfully climbed Big STEPS 1 and 2 yet and you need to go back because you've got work to do!

Whatever the answer turns out to be, it's your job as the director to work with your cast to find the way to deliver to your chosen standard.

Talking of your cast, we believe every productive cast member who is serving customers should be generating four times their hourly basic wage, so an hourly rate of £8 means a target of £32 per hour as a standard as well.

Cast members who fall well below this standard make it difficult to stick to your wages budget and in the end everybody pays a price.

Do you understand what we mean by a standard now? They are incredibly important and hopefully this explanation has helped you see that.

Remember, whatever standards you set ... it's your job as the director to make sure your cast know what's expected and you must also provide the training, measurement and support that makes them consistently achievable.

It's also important that consequences in the form of rewards or penalties have to be implemented ... **fairly and consistently.** We know by now what will happen if this rule is ignored, don't we!

We do see many salon owners get bogged down in organising all this so, *just like we did with **Your Salon is a Stage*** we want to show you a way of making it simple to see WHAT needs to be done.

We call it creating The Customer Journey.

Speak to any theatre director and they'll tell you that designing and putting together the live **'performance'** is only part of the story because good theatres will try and make the whole experience of booking, arriving, watching and leaving, as enjoyable and consistent as possible.

They know a consistent emotionally engaging experience is essential for positive word of mouth to spread like a virus. They know the total package is important.

There has to be a reason why shows like *We Will Rock You* and *Mamma Mia*, which tell stories based on the music of *Queen* and *Abba* run and run, while *Viva Forever* the *Spice Girls* musical based on equally popular music sank without trace.

You might blame the critics for the difference, but *Les Misérables* proves that customers make up their own minds about what they like ... **and word of mouth is what really matters.**

We'll let **Cameron Mackintosh**, the man behind *Les Misérables* explain why.

He says:

"The opening night of Les Misérables at the Barbican Theatre on 8 October 1985 was one of those extraordinary occasions when against all the odds a theatrical alchemy took place that made everyone forget the years of work that went into adapting this sweeping masterpiece for the musical stage."

"The show simply soared that night, and both the audience and cast were elevated to a state of powerful emotion rarely seen in the theatre."

"Intoxicated by the events of the evening, I rushed off to Fleet Street to get the papers. One of the first I read said **"Les Misérables has, sadly, been reduced to The Glums,"** *and my heart sank. I couldn't reconcile the sense of uplift and exhilaration I had witnessed in the theatre with these words."*

"Many of the other papers were equally dismissive. That bleak reaction left me poleaxed."

"About midday I thought I would get all the bad news out of the way and ring the box office to find out how the reviews had affected ticket sales. I was greeted by an incredulous box office manager who wondered how I had managed to get through as they'd been besieged, having already sold a record-breaking 5,000 seats that morning. I was stunned."

"The public had just voted with its feet. Without any media hype or any mass marketing, the public was able to see in 'Les Misérables' what many a professional scribe could not. For me it was a great lesson in the real power of word of mouth and the often under-appreciated sense of perception of the public."

It's a powerful story, isn't it and did you notice the phrase *"one of those extraordinary occasions when against all the odds a theatrical alchemy took place"*?

This is what will happen in your salon when you build 'The 3 BIG Steps'™ into the experience you give your customers.

They have the ability to create a word of mouth tidal wave that will make conventional **'marketing'** almost redundant for you, but we'll get to that a bit later!

So back to The Customer Journey ... we're looking to create systems and processes that allow the whole experience of a visit to the salon to be delivered consistently.

Always ... **Always** ... **ALWAYS** remember your story and the promise it's built on are the foundation for The Customer Journey.

Together they define what your customer should experience and as the director your job is to constantly find amusing, interesting and involving ways of creating, training and constantly refining The Customer Journey with your cast.

We'll say that again!

As the director your job is to constantly find amusing, interesting and involving ways of creating, training and constantly refining The Customer Journey with your cast.

We repeated the words because repetition underpins consistency and consistency is your secret weapon ... but only if you create it in the right way.

Doing it in the right way means making the creation or improvement of The Customer Journey a cast project you **'direct'** rather than something you impose on them like a dictator.

Assuming you're a Salon Owner with an existing salon which already has rules, systems and processes in place, *however ineffective they may be* ... **this is what you do.**

Arrange regular meetings with your cast. If there's one sin we see being committed in salon after salon it's badly run, infrequent or irregular meetings.

If you EVER want to climb Step 3 successfully you need the regular heartbeat of meetings with your cast and you need to make them amusing, interesting and involving.

This is a non-negotiable part of being the director and it involves preparation!

Many successful directors hold mini meetings, *either one to one or whole cast*, every morning or evening. These meetings can be used to make sure the stage is set for the day and everyone understands their goals.

Mini meetings work well if you make them inspiring and motivating. On the days you're not available other cast members could lead them for you, if you train them how to do it.

As an absolute **minimum** you should hold a full cast meeting lasting at least 30 minutes every week. At least part of each meeting should be dedicated to creating or improving The Customer Journey.

Have a plan, a white board or flip chart, any props games or exercises you're going to use and a positive attitude ready to go.

If you're planning a group discussion, split your cast into pairs - or groups of 3. It makes sense to change the pairs or groups regularly to avoid 'meeting cliques' forming.

Start by explaining WHY you're having this meeting.

If anything is going to limit what can be decided, make this information clear.

Once they know WHY they are there and WHAT the rules or limits for discussion are, give them a question to discuss and ask them to go off for 5 minutes in their pairs/ groups to write down their thoughts or answers.

After the 5 minutes is up, get everyone together again and ask each pair/group what they wrote down.

Write all their answers on the white board/flipchart.

Don't judge or comment on what they've given you until you've got everyone's answers ... just thank each pair/group and move on.

When all the answers are on the board, you need to put your director's hat on and lead the process that follows.

First of all, look through the suggestions to see if any miss the point, break the rules or limits you set, or could, from past experience cause problems. If the answer is yes, explain the problem, thank the pair/group again for coming up with the idea, then cross it off the list.

Now go through the answers that are left and ask for opinions about which would work best, or ask if 2 suggestions could be combined to make something better.

Normally what happens is a healthy discussion then follows, the right answer quickly becomes obvious and agreement is reached.

If you have deadlock or no agreement, ask everyone to review all the options and give 3 points to their favourite, 2 points to their second choice and 1 point to their third.

Count up the points each option scores and you should have a clear winner.

Tell everyone you'll get the decision(s) of the meeting typed up neatly in time for next week's meeting.

At the next meeting get everyone to check what's written matches what was decided, and then sign their name to agree to abide by the decision.

The signed piece of paper then goes into the ... **'The Customer Journey Book'** and becomes the way every cast member does it from now on.

If the decision doesn't stick then, as the director you need to investigate and understand **why**. If the problem is down to a poor attitude, it's your job to deal with it. If it's a system issue then take it back to the cast and look at your decision again to see how it can be improved.

It's obvious how doing this would constantly refine and improve the experience of The Customer Journey, isn't it!

By the way, the questions you use **are** important and need to be framed as open questions so they're easy to think about and answer. Here are 10 sample questions we've used with success to give you an idea how to go about it.

1. How do we make sure the phone is answered within 4 rings?

2. How do we make sure customers who call the salon enjoy the experience?

3. How do we make sure customers feel welcome when they arrive at the salon?

4. How do we make sure we find out WHAT a customer WANTS rather than just NEEDS when they are with us?

5. How do we make sure our customers feel special EVERY time they visit?

6. How do we make sure we know our regular customers preferred magazines and refreshments?

7. How do we make sure the salon is clean, organised, and inviting all the time?

8. How do we make sure our gowns and towels always look and feel fresh and new?

9. How do we make sure we never keep a customer waiting?

10. How do we make sure visiting the salon toilet is a delight?

You might like to know that meetings don't have to be group discussions. They can be training sessions in disguise as well. Julie is brilliant at setting up **'experiences'** cast members can learn from.

Here are three examples.

Example 1: The *'Customer Service'* Experience

She split her cast into pairs; put the names of different coffee shops in her town into a hat and each pair drew one at random.

She then got them to think about the experience they were expecting based on their knowledge of the reputation of the coffee shop and share it with her.

Next she gave them the money and time to go and have a coffee at their allocated shop.

Finally, when they came back, a meeting was held where everyone discussed their experience and how it differed from their expectations. The lessons that came out were very powerful and customer service in the salon improved because of it.

Example 2: The *'Spot The Deliberate Mistake'* Experience

There was a time when cleaning was an issue so she

prepared for a meeting by **staging 5 deliberate 'mistakes' in the salon**. These ranged from tools being put back in the wrong place, to debris on the floor and smears on mirrors.

At the start of the meeting she explained what she'd done, offered a **£1 reward** for every deliberate **'mistake'** that was spotted and sent her cast off to search for them.

They found more than 5 ... in the end the total was 10 and everyone learned a powerful lesson! Especially when they discovered that one of the mistakes was a hairpin placed behind the customer toilet door which Julie deliberately put there 3 weeks before ... **that's what we call planning!**

In case you're wondering Julie did pay out £10 rather than the £5 she originally budgeted, because she wanted to reward cast members for doing such a good job spotting things!

Example 3: The '*What Clients Really See*' Experience

Like most good ideas, this one is simple as well. All she did was split her cast into pairs and asked them to go round the salon with a piece of paper and a pen and sit in every seat.

While they were sat down, their task was to look round carefully at EVERYTHING that was visible from that chair, spot what wasn't up to the standards of The Customer Journey and write it down.

Then she got everyone together to compare notes so a definitive 'to do' list could be created **and** her cast got a better view of the customer perspective as well, didn't they.

Now, we accept we're asking you to invest quite a bit of time and money into holding meetings and training sessions with your cast and you might be wondering if it's all worth it.

You'll realise it is, when you learn the shocking fact that fully **68%** of the customers who decide to stop coming to your salon and start going somewhere else do it because they take exception to the attitude, behaviour or performance of just **one** of your cast members!

That's all it takes.

Just **one** cast member to miss something obvious, be in a bad mood, feel negative or be unprofessional and you've lost a customer.

When you understand the real **'lifetime'** cost of losing a customer who comes in regularly you might be motivated to take action!

To make sure you **are** motivated to take action we want you to join us as we go through a thought provoking **'cost of losing a customer'** exercise.

Let's assume an average bill of **£35** and **7** salon visits a year which gives you an average customer value of **£35 x 7** visits = **£245 a year.**

Now let's assume they would have spent the same £245 a year for another 5 years. Add it all together and it comes to **£245 X 5** years = **£1225 *worth of turnover you've lost.***

All because someone was having a bad day and was unprofessional enough to show it!

Multiply your losses by a few hundred customers just

because your cast isn't performing consistently and it's easy to see how your salon can end up constantly needing to market for new clients, isn't it!

Constantly needing to find new clients is a sure sign that Big STEPS 1 and 2 haven't been taken!

Can you see **WHY** it will pay you many times over to create a performance that puts great emphasis on service with a professional attitude **and** consistent delivery of your promise through the whole Customer Journey?

It will pay you because it increases:

- How much a customer will spend.

- How often customers come in.

- How long customers stay loyal to you.

- How ready they are to recommend you to their friends.

Before we look at WHY this happens we promised earlier in the book to show you HOW you can organise your salon so you only do the bits you enjoy doing ... **didn't we!**

The answer is simple.

First of all you make the decision to delegate. It might sound obvious but it constantly amazes us how many salon owners 'wish' things were different but they are afraid to make the decision that they are GOING to be.

This is just 'insecurity virus' thinking!

Once the real intent is there, just make a list of all your responsibilities and use our simple **'splitting method'** to break your list into easy to manage parts that make it clear what needs to happen.

So start with your full list and let's split it into two. Do this by looking at each item and decide if it belongs in Part A: The things you enjoy doing or **Part B:** The things you want done for you.

When you've completed that step just keep **Part A** for yourself and take **Part B** and split it into two separate lists in the same way.

The question you ask to help you decide this time is ... **can my cast do it, or shall I need to find someone from outside?**

Once you've answered that question for every item let's look first at the list of help you want outsiders to provide for you.

We can start by asking ... Would a good computer system help?

When it comes to measuring your casts performance against your standards and also communicating consistently to your customers in a **'connected'** way the right computer system can be invaluable.

As you may have read in the foreword to this book we are happy to recommend the *Phorest System* www.phorest.com to anyone who asks, not just because the software is good, *and it is **very** good*, but particularly because they are great people to do business with.

They are great because their training and support is exceptional and they understand the art of 'connecting' with customers so their system makes retention marketing very easy to do effectively.

If financial management is a challenge for you, it's obvious you've got the wrong accountant.

A good accountant will take the time to understand what you need and organise your financial systems around your strengths, not criticize you for your weaknesses!

They'll also help you understand your figures on a regular basis so you can make any decisions in real time ... not 6 months after it's too late to do anything about it, which is what normally happens.

In our experience far too many accountants offer an appalling service to their customers and most salon owners don't seem to realise this, or if they do they just think all accountants are the same, so there's no point in moving.

This is just madness.

If you'd like to see what an accountant who understands salon owners and can offer a flexible, cost effective service can do for you, take a look at **www.cdcaccounting.com** which is run by Chris Cheeney who is married to a salon owner, so he really does understand what we're like ... **and what we want!**

More and more of the salon owners we work with are using him and they seem very happy!

Does the thought of sorting out and maintaining your

web site plus your social media and online directory presence cause you sleepless nights?

If it does, then go to **www.imahairsalon.co.uk** where you'll find they offer a cost effective all inclusive service for salon owners. They are very friendly and helpful so have a look and see what you think.

These are just some of the people **we** know who can help you take control and get things done, but quite often if you ask around you'll find **you** have a customer or family member who does what you want and you can barter salon services for their time and expertise!

We've used this method to get photography, video creation, decorating, plumbing, newsletter writing and web site creation done in the past.

For anything you can't get done by barter, the next question to ask is does the person doing the job need to physically be at the salon to do it for me *(like decorating or plumbing)* or can it be done virtually anywhere *(like newsletter writing or web site creation)*.

If they need to physically be at the salon, then tap your contacts again for good people. If it can be done virtually, then go to sites like **www.elance.com** or **www.fiverr.co.uk** where you'll find a whole army of people who will be happy to bid for the chance to do just about any job for you that you can imagine.

Everyone who submits a bid will have testimonials and a star rating provided by previous customers ... **so it's quite safe for you to find people this way.**

Yes there will be a cost for employing outsiders to help

you, but choose the right people and the jobs will be done properly, plus you'll be free to do what you love doing and do best ... which is priceless!

What do you do if you want your cast to take on the task?

Systems help here, which means breaking each task into smaller easy to do 'chunks' ... just like they do at McDonald's.

If needed:

- Be prepared to get expert help or training for your cast members.

- Also create a supportive atmosphere while they are learning and improving.

- Finally be prepared to show your appreciation for what they are doing, especially if they are going outside their comfort zone to help you.

This might all sound scary, but we're not suggesting you do anything we haven't done ourselves.

Simon created a very busy salon that took only a couple of hours a week of his time to lead and employed no manager.

In his salon the day to day performance and management of every single task, *except accounting*, was performed by very normal girls who were all trained hairdressers. They were happy to take on additional responsibilities because they belonged to a cast that was passionate about keeping their promise.

To be specific, we're talking about tasks as different as interviewing, health and safety, book keeping, stock purchase, newsletter writing, marketing and so on.

They did it all and only brought Simon in when they thought it was helpful. Of course he kept an eye on the numbers, got involved when issues occurred, but once all the systems were in place you'd be surprised how rarely it was necessary.

All this happened by following the principles we've set out in this book for you. He'll tell you himself, he's not a naturally organised person; he's not even a great manager ... **so he's not the magic ingredient that made his salon run like this.**

All he did was understand and apply the principles we've set out in this book.

Trust us ... *if he can do it, so can you!*

Chapter 8

What Could Be Better!

A few minutes ago we looked at the cost of losing a customer and suggested it would be more rewarding to help them do the following instead:

- Spend more.
- Come in more frequently.
- Stay loyal for longer.
- Feel happy to recommend you.

These four simple things are the key to growing your business.

It's true ... Just think about it and you'll see that EVERYTHING we've shared with you in this book has been coming to this point.

We've Been Giving You The Secret To Long Term Success!

- ✓ By starting with WHY and understanding the truth about 'insecurity' we've made it easier for your customers and cast members to trust you, connect with you and feel confident following you.

- ✓ By understanding your passion and turning it into a purpose with a powerful promise, we've made

145

your salon stand out like a beacon in a crowded market place.

✓ By taking your promise and turning it into an **'emotional experience'** that can be delivered as a **'performance'** just like they do in great theatres we've created a model that introduces consistency.

✓ By showing you how to recognise and create a cast that identifies with your purpose and promise, we've given you the support you need keep your promise.

✓ By showing you how be a director who can lead effectively, we've given you the tools to bring the best out in your cast.

✓ By showing you how to get your salon organised and create **'The Customer Journey'**, we've given you the tools to deliver a consistent performance, time after time.

✓ By showing you the cost of getting it wrong, we hope we've given you the motivation to want to do it right!

It's been a journey for all of us, hasn't it!

We've asked you to think about and face up to some challenging concepts that are certainly outside your comfort zone, or *you'd have been doing them already* and it's all been building up to this point.

Now we want to show you what happens to a salon when you get it all right!

We're going to do it by taking the figures from our **'cost of losing a customer'** exercise and all we need to do is flip them into reverse!

This means instead of losing customers and turnover, the opposite happens ... **you keep your customers and they spend more!**

Oh we almost forgot, they come in more often, stay loyal for longer and recommend you to their friends as well ... **and do all this because they want to!**

Are you ready!

If you remember we suggested in the last exercise that your average customer was worth **£1225** to your salon.

Let's also assume you currently have **1000** regular customers, this means the total potential value of all your customers would be **£1225 X 1000 = £1,225,000**

What happens if as part of delivering The Customer Journey, you and your cast members get into character and clear your minds, so you're truly there **'in the moment'** to serve her? Preparing like this makes it easy to hear the words she uses when she's telling you about her frustrations, problems, wants and needs during her consultation, doesn't it!

By the way the difference between a NEED and a WANT is profound.

A need is just WHAT needs to be done and a customer has very little emotional attachment to it. Meeting her needs isn't going to turn anyone into a raving fan, long term loyal customer.

A want is a very different thing. There's a reason WHY she want's what she wants and that reason is often loaded with emotion.

Tap into her WHY and reflect her **'emotional'** words back to her when you're presenting your SOLUTION and your customer will know you've listened and are now offering a personalised answer that gives her what she REALLY wants.

By the way, living and breathing the word **solution** is very important which is why we emphasised it.

Providing solutions to customer's problems is very different from the dreaded 'selling' scenario that most salon owners try and force down their reluctant cast member and customers throats.

Why is it different?

Because there's no pressure! Your customer just sees someone who is trying to help and all that happens is that the quality of the connection between them and your cast members goes up.

Selling has the opposite affect ... it drives customers away!

So think about it.

If you're offering your customer what she really wants and you're doing it in a way that's not pressured is she likely to spend more in your salon or less?

More of course ... **A LOT MORE!**

Let's assume her average bill goes up to **£43** what happens to the numbers?

£43 X 7 visits a year X 5 years X 1000 customers = £1,505,000 which means the total value of all your clients has gone up by **£280,000** over the next **5** years, which is a lot, isn't it.

Let's look at what happens if, *by doing exactly what we just described to find out what your customer REALLY wants and offering solutions*, you end up introducing additional new services like hair extensions, smoothing services, laser treatments, body wraps or any other professional problem solving solutions you may decide to offer.

Is a **'connected'** customer more likely or less likely to come in more frequently if she's enjoying these additional services?

More likely of course!

Let's assume she now comes in **8** times a year and spends **£43**

£43 x 8 visits a year X 5 years X 1000 customers = £1,720,000 and the total value of all your customers has risen by a total of **£495,000** over the next **5** years.

Once again this increase would be delivered with no new customers at all ... instead it comes from inspiring and training your cast to perform with a professional attitude towards delivering your promise through The Customer Journey ... **and we haven't finished yet!**

Let's assume when we get into character and clear our minds, so we're truly there **'in the moment'** and listening well, we can really **HEAR** what our customers are telling us about their preferences and what's going on in their lives.

Important things to them like:

- How they like their coffee.

- Their favourite magazines.

- When their birthday is.

- The fact they're going to be a grandparent.

- That they've been into hospital for some tests.

- That their husband just left them.

- That they were taking their driving test.

This list isn't exhaustive it's just typical of the things we learn about customers every day. The power comes from remembering it all!

Let's assume we're professional enough to create a record of what we hear in a customer's file and remind ourselves of their preferences and news just before we see them again.

Let's assume we're professional enough to use the information to conjure up **'magic moments of connection'** with customers by caring enough to be creative with how we introduce what we've remembered into the conversation.

Do you think your customer is more likely or less likely to stay loyal to your salon?

More likely of course! Our research shows that customers of professional salons like the one we're describing here stay loyal on average for **10 years** instead of **5** so let's see what that does to the value of the same **1000** customers we started this exercise with.

£43 X 8 times a year X 10 years X 1000 = £3,440,000 or an increase in value of **£2,215,000** to your salon turnover and if you divide that sum by **£1225** the lifetime value of the original customer we started this exercise with you'd discover the following amazing fact.

You'd have had to find **1808** new customers spending **£1225** to make the same increase in value.

Which would you rather do ... look after your existing customers more professionally or find 1808 new ones?

Now we haven't finished yet.

- We've been professional.

- We've listened.

- We've understood what our customers really want.

- We've recommended solutions that have solved their problems.

- We've created magic moments of connection that make them feel noticed, understood, connected and special.

- We've done all this consistently because it's delivering our promise and your whole cast is committed to doing it.

Think about it ... are your customers more likely or less likely to trust you enough to recommend their friends?

More likely of course!

Let's assume your 1000 customers each recommend 2 friends a year who stay loyal, that's 20 friends each and 20,000 new customers in all ... *who have the potential to spend nearly £69 million pounds in your salons (we say salons because you'll never fit them all into one!)* ... **without you spending a penny on advertising for a single new customer!**

Can you see why **'The 3 BIG Steps'™** we're sharing with you in this book are so powerful?

Can you see that we've just shown you how to make your salon marketing ridiculously easy?

Do everything we've suggested and word of mouth will attract all the customers and cast members you'll ever need in a mind blowing way.

Please understand that marketing tools like your newlsetters, your website and Social Media are important but only in as far as they help develop and spread word of mouth momentum.

You just have to stick to the fundamentals and make sure you:

✓ Connect with your customers.

- ✓ Listen to what they WANT.
- ✓ Deliver consistently.
- ✓ Make them feel special.

Do all this and you'll give them a story to tell themselves and their friends. **Do it consistently and they'll also make Social Media work for you.**

By all means give your customers a helping hand to take word of mouth viral by providing interesting education, enjoyable events and engaging stories in your newsletter, on your web site and social media channels for them to like and share.

By all means use PR and media opportunities, to tell the story of your WHY and spark even more word of mouth conversations.

By all means support local charities and give back to the community that supports your business ... **because you're in the business of connection and serving.**

We haven't mentioned discounts or special offers quite deliberately. Why not? Because you could see them both as bribery and manipulation in disguise!

Human nature being it what it is, bribery and manipulation **will** give you effective short term results, but think about it ... **does bribing someone to recommend a friend, try a new service, like your Facebook page or vote for you in your local papers 'salon of the year' competition where the results can easily be rigged, really increase connection, confidence**

and trust in you in the long term?

We don't think so!

And what do you really want ...

- **A cut price customer for today.**

- **Or a love who you are and what you stand for 'Customer For Life'?**

The answers obvious, isn't it!

CHAPTER 9

WHAT'S NEXT?

We promised you a book with the secret to long term success at its heart and **Customers For Life** is that secret.

We believe we've kept our promise but when you think about it we hope you'll see it's been a book about so much more than that.

Think back to the questions we asked on the very first page of the introduction.

- WHY does my salon exist?

- WHY should my staff choose to work with me, stay loyal to me, or care about me and my business enough to invest their careers in helping me grow it?

- WHY should a customer choose my salon to care about, be loyal to, to become a raving fan of?

The answer to all these questions is ... FOR THE LIFE IT GIVES.

Your salon exists to give life to your passion, your purpose and your promise.

Your staff will choose you because you give them so much more than a job. You give **them** life, passion and purpose with your trust, respect, passion, purpose and promise.

Your customers will choose your salon because in an ever

more stressful world where nobody seems to have time, you bring them to life simply by listening, noticing and caring enough to give them what they really want ... connection and somewhere where they matter.

All this comes from understanding **'The 3 BIG Steps'™** and applying the knowledge they share.

But do you remember Julies quote ... ***"Knowledge is power but only when you use it!"***

Because of STEP 1 you know ...

WHY

- ✓ WHY your 'insecurity virus' is just an illusion you can either deal with logically through Stage Climbing or intuitively with The 3 Principles and the inside out revolution.

- ✓ WHY achieving this allows you to finally answer your big WHY questions and polish your *3 Ps ... your Passion, your Purpose and your Promise ...* into a compelling emotionally attractive story.

Because of STEP 2 you know ...

HOW

- ✓ HOW 'Your Salon Is A stage' makes the ideal strategy for delivering the performance of your customer promise, consistently in a way that emotionally engages everyone.

- ✓ HOW to identify the ideal cast members for your

production and move on any who might not be right for you.

- ✓ HOW to become a leader who is capable of directing a great performance in a way that connects with both cast and customers.

Because of STEP 3 you know ...

WHAT

- ✓ WHAT creates the perfect Customer Journey; **remember 'It's the little things that count!'**

- ✓ WHAT systems, processes measurement and standards will be needed to deliver a consistent performance.

- ✓ WHAT to do to get the help you need when you need it!

- ✓ WHAT makes WHY + HOW = What a great salon!

You have knowledge but as we've already explained there's only so much we can put in a book like this, and you might want more.

More than knowledge you might want help applying what you've discovered to your own unique, individual, very special salon and this is why we've created **'The 3 BIG Steps Courses'™**

You already know about:

- • **'Climbing Big Step 1 ... Revealing Your WHY.'** This course is for you if you want some practical support dealing with any insecurity issues. Helpful exercises for revealing your purpose, understanding your story and the promise you can make at the heart of it.

- **'Climbing Step 2 ... Developing Your HOW.'** This course is for you if you want some practical cast developing skills, like interviewing, running effective meetings and turning yourself into a leader your cast are happy to follow.

Now you won't be surprised to learn there's a third course:

- **'Climbing Step 3 ... Organising Your WHAT.'** This course is for you if you truly want to create an amazing **Customer Journey,** get your salon well organised and deliver a nonstop conveyor belt of **Customers For Life!**

Many courses are available on line these days but all our research shows that you learn a lot more and learn it more quickly at live events where you can engage with other salon owners **and** can be held to account to do the exercises.

This is why we've combined all 3 courses together to create our 3 day, intensive **'3 BIG STEPS WORKSHOP'** that has the power to make our promise of **'Customers For Life'** your life changing reality!

Taking part is fun, interactive, packed with opportunities to learn and its risk free because every **'3 BIG STEPS WORKSHOP'** ticket is protected by our 100% money back **'Absolute Happiness Guarantee'.**

But before you even think about attending a live event we want to send you your own **FREE 'Customers For Life Pack'** which normally sells for **£247/€247** because it will help you get so much more from this book AND give you a real taste of what you can expect from a '3 BIG STEPS WORKSHOP.'

It contains:

- ✓ An **mp3 audiobook** version of **'The Salon Owners Bible'** worth £20.00/€20.00

- ✓ A **3 DVD** set of edited highlights from a live '3 BIG STEPS WORKSHOP' worth £197/€197.00

- ✓ **1 months FREE membership** of **'The Successful Salon Club'** worth **£30.00/€30.00**

The audiobook is read by Simon and he really brings **'The Salon Owners Bible'** alive. It allows you to learn the secret to attracting **'Customers For Life'** while you're driving your car or commuting to work.

The **DVD** set is amazing. Three salon owners volunteered to take part in an intimate, specially filmed edition of this ground breaking workshop. Watch and you'll see them learn, laugh and cry as they finally realise they can take control of their salons and achieve what they really want!

Finally your 1 month's membership of **'The Successful Salon Club'** gives you a taste of our long term commitment to helping you create and maintain a successful salon. As a member, every month a **CD and printed Newsletter** packed with powerful advice, strategies and lessons from some of the industry's most successful leaders will arrive through the post. There's also a **'Business Advice Hotline'** for members and most important of all up to **40% discount off tickets for all our live events and working one to one with Julie and Simon.**

All this truly is yours for **FREE** and all you have to do to get it is go to www.CustomersForLifePack.com and tell us where to send your pack.

We'll do the rest!